ORGANISING
MUSIC
IN LIBRARIES

ORGANISING
MUSIC
IN LIBRARIES

VOLUME ONE
Arrangement and Classification

BRIAN REDFERN

CLIVE BINGLEY
LONDON

LINNET BOOKS
HAMDEN · CONN

FIRST PUBLISHED 1966
THIS REVISED AND REWRITTEN EDITION PUBLISHED 1978
BY CLIVE BINGLEY LTD
16 PEMBRIDGE ROAD LONDON W11 UK
SIMULTANEOUSLY PUBLISHED IN THE USA BY LINNET BOOKS
AN IMPRINT OF THE SHOE STRING PRESS INC
995 SHERMAN AVENUE HAMDEN CONNECTICUT 06514
SET IN 10 ON 12 POINT PRESS ROMAN BY ALLSET
PRINTED AND BOUND IN THE UK BY REDWOOD BURN LTD
TROWBRIDGE AND ESHER
COPYRIGHT © BRIAN REDFERN 1978
ALL RIGHTS RESERVED
BINGLEY ISBN: 0 85157 231 6
LINNET ISBN: 0 208 01544 2

Library of Congress Cataloging in Publication Data

Redfern, Brian L
    Organising music in libraries.

    Bibliography: v. 1, p.
    CONTENTS: v. 1. Arrangement and classification.
    1. Music libraries.   2. Classification—Music.
3. Cataloging of music.   4. Cataloging of phono-
records. I. Title.
ML111.R4   1978   025.3'4'8   78-819
ISBN 0-208-05144-2

CONTENTS

Preface   7

Glossary and abbreviations   8

Chapter One   Problems of organising material   9

Chapter Two   Special schemes   23

Chapter Three   Treatment of music in some general schemes of classification   49

Chapter Four   A special scheme for jazz   83

Chapter Five   The classification of musical instruments   87

Chapter Six   The arrangement of sound recordings   93

Chapter Seven   Conclusion   97

Further reading   99

Index   102

PREFACE

THIS REVISED EDITION of *Organising music in libraries* will appear in two volumes. This first one is entirely concerned with questions of arrangement and classification, the second (to appear late 1978 or early 1979) will deal with cataloguing and bibliographic control. The main reason for this two-volume format is to take advantage of the predicted publication in 1978 of the second edition of the Anglo-American Cataloguing Rules.

The book is still intended primarily for students, but the number of schemes discussed has been increased and the original text considerably revised. It is hoped that practising librarians may therefore find something of value in its pages.

The dedication remains to those who have laboured to compile the schemes discussed. I hope others will be stimulated, by what I have written, to a further study of them.

I am grateful to many colleagues and friends both at the Polytechnic of North London and in the International Association of Music Libraries, who have contributed ideas and shaped my thoughts. I hope anyone with comments and ideas will write to me at the address below, as I am always interested and happy to discuss the problems of organising music in libraries.

School of Librarianship
The Polytechnic of North London
207-225 Essex Road
London N1 3PN

Brian Redfern
Principal Lecturer

GLOSSARY

Compound subject: a subject composed of two or more basic elements derived from different categories or groups of terms eg 'piano concerto' is a compound subject of *piano* and *concerto* taken respectively from the categories (**facets**, qv) instruments and form.

Expressive notation : one which reveals the structure of the subject as arranged by the classification.

Facet: a group of subdivisions of a subject, all of which have a common feature, which only the members of that group possess and which gives its name to that group, eg a facet of music is 'instrument', all the sub-divisions in this group having the common characteristic of being the medium by which the music is produced by the performer.

Focus: a sub-division within a facet, eg 'piano' is a focus within the facet 'instrument'.

Literature: books about music.

Music: scores.

Phase relationship: a relationship between two main classes of knowledge, eg music and religion.

Score: a musical work in manuscript or printed form, generally used for works for two or more performers. A *full score* is a complete score, containing all the parts, instrumental and/or vocal, fully set out. A *miniature score* is a reduction of a full score. A *vocal score* consists of the original vocal parts with a reduction for keyboard of the orchestral parts.

ABBREVIATIONS

BC	Bliss Bibliographic Classification
BCM	British Catalogue of Music Classification
DC	Dewey Decimal Classification
IAML	International Association of Music Libraries
LC	Library of Congress Classification
UDC	Universal Decimal Classification

CHAPTER ONE

PROBLEMS OF ORGANISING MATERIAL

THE TASK before a librarian is a very simple one. On the one hand, there is an item containing 'information'. On the other hand, there is a person who needs that information. The librarian must do all that is necessary to ensure that as speedily as possible the item is made available to the reader.

Difficulties begin to arise as soon as the library holds more than one item or that item happens to contain complex information, which cannot be easily summarised or is capable of being differently interpreted by two persons. If the library has more than one item a sequence must be found for the arrangement of the items and the reader must understand that order, if direct access to the items is allowed. If the information is complex, some system of indexing it must be devised to cater for different approaches. Thus a collection of piano music presents a fairly simple indexing problem, but a trio for flute, horn and viola implies at least three possible subject approaches.

The problems arising from sequence or order are very closely related to those stemming from the need for indexes. If the two items above are being arranged in a sequence under instruments, then the first item can be easily arranged under *piano*, which is where the user will expect to find it. But if the second item is arranged under *flute*, then the approaches through *horn* and *viola* can only be met by devising an index. It might also be necessary to cater for *trio*. In fact the item might be arranged under this as the primary sought term.

Music librarians have generally claimed that the problems relating to music are essentially different from those met in handling other materials, particularly books, and that a basic knowledge of music and ability to read a score are essential prerequisites for the cataloguer and classifier of music. The second volume will demonstrate the truth of this claim as far as cataloguing is concerned, but in the case of classification or order there is some evidence to suggest that, certainly as far as devising a scheme for arrangement is concerned, a good grounding in classification principles may be of more value. Ideally, a musician who understands and can apply the theory of classification is needed. Whatever knowledge is brought to the problem of organising music in a library, there must be a solution which will provide an order on the shelves making sense to the users of the library and arranging material in a helpful and systematic way; while, if the items have compound subjects, indexes must be provided to cater for secondary, alternative approaches.

This volume is concerned solely with the question of order, although because of its close relationship to the problems of arrangement, some mention is made of subject indexing in so far as it relates to individual schemes. This chapter, being introductory, also contains references in very general terms to all aspects of cataloguing.

Since the first edition there have been developments in the area of classification as well as those currently proceeding in cataloguing and indexing which will be discussed in volume two. Probably the most important in terms of the immediate effect on music libraries is the work which has been done on providing new schedules for the arrangement of music in the Dewey Decimal Classification (DC) and the Bliss Classification (BC). These will both be fully discussed, but it should be noted here that both of them are firmly based in their different ways on the order devised by Eric Coates for the British Catalogue of Music Classification (BCM). At the present time it is uncertain whether the new schedules will be used in DC, but those for BC will definitely be used. This means that the theories of faceted classification, which will be fully explained below, have now been recognised as having major significance for the arrangement of music by their use for the full scale revision of BC, which is in course of publication, and by their likely use for the music class in DC.

It is interesting to speculate on the reasons for the large number of schemes which exist for the arrangement of music in libraries and bibliographies. Maureen Long in her research for *Musicians and libraries in the United Kingdom* (London, Library Association, 1972) discovered not only that each of the published schemes was used either in its original or a modified form, but also that many music libraries had developed their own schedules. This suggests that there is much dissatisfaction with the published schemes and particularly with DC, which is undoubtedly the most widely used general scheme. But subject specialists in other areas of knowledge have expressed dissatisfaction with the arrangement of their subjects in DC without necessarily going on to produce their own schemes. Perhaps this has occurred more in music because the

10

material has a different physical format and frequently a separate music department has been established. Whatever the reason there is certainly much interest amongst music librarians in the problems of organising their libraries.

Undoubtedly part of this arises from the intractable nature of the material, once consideration is given to the variety of formats in which music is published and the vast range of instrumentation for which it has been written. Since the publication of the first edition of this book one of the major developments in library science has been the application of computers to the management of libraries. The full potential of these subtle machines has yet to be realised, but it is apparent and proven that they will provide a limitless approach to the knowledge contained in libraries, their capacity for storage being limited only by the information which is fed into them in the first place. It could well be therefore that within a very short time music libraries will arrange their material on the shelves in a very simple order and use computers to provide all kinds of complex and sophisticated approaches to the items so arranged.

Parallel with this development of the use of computers there has been a growing reaction to some of the more abstruse classification theories and a growing feeling in some quarters that very specific classification of individual items may not be the best answers to users' needs. Economic considerations also enter here, as generally the more specific the classification the longer the practical process of classifying is likely to take. Although to classify by BCM, one of the most detailed schemes, is much easier and more consistently reliable than classification by DC or Library of Congress (LC), both of which lack the specificity provided by BCM.

Perhaps the fundamental problem with classification is that it has always been assumed by librarians to be necessary without enough examination of its effect on users of libraries, the value they place on it and its cost-effectiveness in making material accessible. Indeed some schemes could be accused of making material inaccessible. A good example of this would be the obscure slots which jazz and popular music have been allocated in most schemes, and to which further reference will be made in discussing individual classifications.

Nevertheless order is necessary in libraries and careful consideration must be given to the various factors which affect that order. There are four with which the music librarian must be concerned: money, time, people, and material. As far as this book is concerned the last two require most attention, but the factors of money and time should not be neglected, for they affect the quantity and quality of any service.

11

Money

Most libraries depend on public funds for their money, which usually means a fairly tight budgetary control. This can be a useful limiting factor, preventing librarians who are too concerned with theory from letting their ideas control their practice to too great an extent.

Unfortunately it can also mean that many good schemes for the development of services are never realised. It is important therefore to examine *all* library activities to ensure that funds are used wisely. Before starting any catalogue of music two questions should be asked: 'How much is it going to cost?' and 'Is it worth it?' In answering the first, the cost of staff as well as the cost of equipment must be remembered. Sometimes the staff cost of cataloguing and classification is hidden in the total cost of all staff in an establishment, but, if possible, component staff costs should always be carefully estimated.

The answer to the second question depends on a very simple rule: *If the library will function properly without a catalogue, then one need not be provided.* Working from this basic rule librarians can decide what additional information they need to provide above that given by the order in which material is arranged on the shelves. For example, if all enquiries for scores use the name of the composer as search term and the scores are arranged alphabetically by composer, there is little point in providing a catalogue arranged by form. The shelves give all the information needed.

In deciding what additional information to provide in the catalogue only general and frequent enquiries should be considered. Attempting to anticipate all possible types of enquiry only results in confusion and waste of money. A good catalogue is intended to be used frequently and to answer questions which occur regularly. Published bibliographies can often be used to supply answers to infrequent forms of enquiry.

Time

Catalogues are expensive items in terms of time. Not only does the initial compilation occupy a lot of staff output, but also the maintenance of, for example, authors' names or correct subject terminology can consume more time than is sometimes realised. This problem is not confined to scientific libraries, as is sometimes suggested. Most libraries, except those concerned with the preservation of material, have to remove records for material which has been lost or withdrawn. Therefore the basic rule on catalogue provision cited above should be the point of commencement. From it an estimate can be made of the time likely to be involved in providing a catalogue of real value.

This question of time needs especially to be taken into account if a decision has to be made as to whether to provide an additional catalogue. Many catalogues have been started with the best intention of giving an extra service, but after a short period they are found to be too costly in terms of time and abandoned. 'We never find time to keep it up to date' is the excuse often made. It is much better not to provide a service at all than to offer one and then take it away.

People

The second fundamental rule for all cataloguers is: *The reader is the most important person to consider.*

Before arranging the material, and the catalogues to it, a careful analysis must be made of readers' needs. Only after this has been done and the material itself analysed, can arrangement and cataloguing proceed.

The readers and the content of the material in the library are the factors which determine the best order to be selected from the many available. It is important to remember that if all the usual enquiries are to be met satisfactorily, the librarian may require certain information which he may use to help the reader, but which the latter never needs. A simple example is the accession number, which is often provided on a catalogue entry. A more complex example is the name of the publisher, which to a good librarian can sometimes be a clue to the authority of the book.

Music librarians, like other subject specialists, are faced with special problems in considering the needs of their readers, for there are many different ways in which music and music literature can be approached. Not all libraries include in their readership all the most common types, but we need to consider all classes of reader here.

The following is a list of main reader categories with examples of the approach each may make. It must be appreciated that individuals cannot be pigeon-holed in this way. One man in his time will play many parts. We are separating the parts.

1 *Musicologists or research workers* Their approach may well be simply by composer. Research having been done in reference books, they probably know what is wanted. However, they might find that an historical order provokes new ideas and needs.

2 *Instrumentalists* This category of reader generally prefers material to be arranged by instrument. Form may also prove a useful arranging device.

3 *Music teachers* Arrangement according to degree of difficulty might

prove most serviceable here, though once again instrument could be an important factor.

4 *Groups of players, singers, etc* Here an approach might depend on the number of people involved. It is interesting to note that *String music in print* (New York, London, Bowker, 2nd ed 1973) arranges primarily by the number of instruments.

5 *General readers and students* The most difficult group to analyse. They may require many different approaches and find the one which the librarian selects unsatisfactory.

6 *Readers who borrow discs and cassettes* This is a comparatively new group, whose main approach for classical music is probably by composer but a new factor here, certainly in popular music, is the performing artist or orchestra. Records will be discussed in chapter six as a separate item.

Material

We have to consider, finally, the material to be arranged. Once we have analysed this and seen what elements exist in the kinds of material a music library stocks, we can group the elements together according to their degrees of likeness. These groups will provide the categories by which our material can be arranged.

A note of confusion can creep in here, which can be best avoided by adopting the simple technical terms proposed by Dr Ranganathan. This eminent Indian librarian is owed a debt of gratitude for the simplicity of his approach to problems in classification, and his work will be discussed at several points throughout this book. Definitions of these terms will be found in the glossary on page 8.

To decide the best order to use in arranging a library, we must examine a quantity of the material and break each title down into elements. This examination of material should continue until no new *facets* are obviously being revealed. This could be after the examination of as few as two hundred titles. It is not proposed to analyse as many titles as this here, only to use sufficient titles to demonstrate the method.

The first five titles will help students to understand the technique. After that they should attempt to analyse the remaining titles themselves before checking their answers against those given below.

1 A companion to Mozart's piano concertos. *Foci*: Mozart/piano/concertos/literature.

2 The Oxford school harmony course. *Foci*: schools/harmony/literature.

3 The sonata (form) in the classic era. *Foci*: sonata form/classic era/literature.

14

4 Prokofiev *Symphony no 6* miniature score. *Foci*: Prokofiev/symphony/ orchestra/score.

5 Bach *Sonata no 2 for solo violin*. *Foci*: Bach/sonata/solo/violin/score.

It is immediately obvious that certain foci belong to the same facet, eg Mozart, Prokofiev, Bach; whereas the focus *solo*, while not belonging to the same group as any other focus so far isolated, may well suggest the facet to which it ultimately belongs, if its nature is considered.

To simplify matters students will find it convenient to use a separate slip of paper or card for each facet and to list the appropriate foci on each slip as they occur in the titles below. It should be emphasised that these titles have been selected to arrive at a quick analysis. In normal circumstances with titles selected at random all the facets would not be so quickly revealed. The remaining titles are:

6 Selected songs by Schubert for high voice—score

7 Mozart *Clarinet quintet* — score and parts

8 The symphonies of Sibelius — a study

9 Bartok's piano concertos — study scores

10 Haydn's string quartets — study scores

11 Vaughan Williams *Romance for viola and piano* — score

12 Haydn *Mass in time of war* — full score

13 Mozart's operas — study

14 Strict tempo dance arrangements

15 Film music of the thirties — arranged for piano

16 A selection of folk songs arranged for four part choir

17 Modes for folk singers

18 Bach's use of counterpoint in his fugues

19 A thematic catalogue of Beethoven's works

20 A dictionary of church music

21 The influence of architecture on the music of Gabrieli

22 Teach yourself to compose music

23 Orchestration in Italian operas

24 Musical aesthetics

25 The effect of climate on Irish pipes

26 The physics of music

Some of these titles are easy to analyse but others present difficulties. We may have to abandon initial ideas not only in our analysis, but also in our grouping into categories. The suggested analyses:

6 selection/songs/high voice/Schubert/score

7 Mozart/clarinet/quintet/ensemble/score

8 symphonies/Sibelius/literature

9 Bartok/piano/concerto/scores
10 Haydn/strings/quartets/ensembles/scores
11 Vaughan Williams/viola/piano/duo/score
12 Haydn/mass/score
13 Mozart/operas/literature
14 tempo/dance/arrangements
15 films/thirties/arrangements/piano/score
16 folk/songs/arrangements/four parts/choir/score
17 modes/folk/voices/literature
18 Bach/counterpoint/fugue/literature
19 catalogue/themes/Beethoven/literature
20 dictionary/church/literature
21 architecture/Gabrieli/literature
22 composition/literature
23 orchestration/Italy/operas/literature
24 aesthetics/literature
25 climate/Irish/pipes/literature
26 physics/literature

The resulting categories are:

facet one	*facet two*	*facet three*
literature	composition	Italy
scores	orchestration	Irish

facet four	*facet five*	*facet six*
architecture	classic era	catalogues
climate	thirties	dictionaries
		selections

facet seven	*facet eight*	*facet nine*
harmony	schools	solo
tempo	dance	quintet
modes	films	duo
counterpoint	folk	quartet
themes	church	four part

facet ten	*facet eleven*	*facet twelve*
concertos	piano	Mozart
symphonies	viola	Prokofiev
sonatas	high voice	Bach
songs	orchestra	Schubert

facet ten (cont)	facet eleven (cont)	facet twelve (cont)
masses	clarinet	Sibelius
operas	ensemble	Bartok
	strings	Haydn
	choir	Vaughan Williams
	pipes	Beethoven
		Gabrieli

facet thirteen	facet fourteen	
sonata form	aesthetics	
fugues	physics	(arrangements)

One point is immediately apparent from this analysis. The music librarian has to contend not only with the literature on the subject, but also with the raw material itself. Ideally it would be best to have literature dealing with the music arranged in the same place on the shelves as the scores, but it will be realised that this presents difficulties of a practical kind owing to the format of scores. A further point is that the music is presented in many different formats such as sheet music (example no 11), full score (no 12), score and parts (no 7), and miniature score (no 4). These physical forms used for the publication of music differ considerably from each other according to their purpose and cannot be satisfactorily arranged in one sequence. Full and miniature scores will contain the same music, the latter often being a photographic reduction of the former, but to place them side by side on the same shelf would mean valuable space being wasted and the frequent disappearance of miniature scores behind the larger volumes. Therefore, before we begin to consider the essential characteristics of the material, we have to recognise that for practical purposes it is better to separate the scores from the literature and to arrange the scores according to format.

It is also possible that some of the facets our examination has revealed may not belong to both literature and music. This is confirmed by checking the items which revealed a particular facet. For example *facet seven*, which groups together the elements a composer may use in composing music, has foci appearing in items 2, 14, 17, 18, 19. All these items are literature and in fact it is extremely unlikely that music would be sought under such terms as 'harmony', 'counterpoint' and 'tempo'. Even collections of examples of such elements will probably be better classified with the literature, for it is with the study of the subject that they really belong.

Other facets which appear in the literature only are *two* (questions of technique), *four* (other subjects outside music), *six* (forms of presentation) and *fourteen* (theory of music). There may be others which we shall decide are best used only in connection with the literature, but those so far considered are probably limited to it.

Firstly it is necessary to settle which facets are important in any arrangement of the music. These are *nine* (size of ensemble), *ten* (musical form), *eleven* (instrument) and *twelve* (composer). These can all be seen to be equally important for the arrangement of the literature.

This leaves several facets to be considered.

Facet three This can be called a geographical or space facet. It must be considered as a possible method of arrangement and will certainly need to be expressed in many divisions of the literature, where studies of the music of geographical areas abound. It is doubtful whether the music needs to be arranged by the space facet, however, as this is not a primary retrieval term for music except in special cases such as folk music or Italian opera; in the latter case this represents a style of composition rather than a geographical entity.

Facet five This provides the historical approach and could be very important for the musicologist, as we have seen. But, once again, while it will need to be expressed in arranging literature where there are many historical studies, it is doubtful whether in general it will be needed for music.

Facet eight This is an interesting group. It is difficult to find a satisfactory name for it, as these foci all represent purposes for which music has been written. BCM uses the term 'musical character', which seems as satisfactory as any. It could be used in arranging both literature and scores, although as far as the latter is concerned some foci will be more important than others. It would seem useful to show what music has been composed for schools, for example, but perhaps not so necessary to separate music for the dance.

Facet thirteen This is very close to musical form and might well form one group. It would appear to be important in both literature and music. In relation to musical form it can be said that those foci isolated in *ten* represent the larger forms, while those in *thirteen* are the smaller forms. Sonata form may be used in concertos, symphonies, masses and operas as well as in sonatas. Some forms, such as rondo form, may appear in either facet. It is possible that some of the smaller forms will not need expression in arranging scores. Examples are first movement or sonata form, binary and ternary forms.

To sum up, the facets to be considered in arranging the literature are: composers, instruments, forms, techniques, elements, musical character, size of ensemble, theory, period or history, space or geographical area, form of presentation, other subjects influencing music. This last is really part of what is called a *phase relationship* and is better so defined.

These facets can be divided into two groups. Some of them are very general in their nature and because we tend to approach subjects in a general way first we would expect them to appear first in any arrangement. These are theory, phase relationship, history, techniques, form of presentation, geographical area. The others are more specific and are composers, instruments, forms, elements, musical character, size of ensemble.

The order of facets in the second group will vary from library to library and depend on the kind of information readers require. It is not possible to say which of the possible permutations is best. The choice must depend on a given situation. In a library where study of the composer is the primary concern we would expect to find literature arranged first by the composer facet, followed possibly by form and then by instrument, but in another situation the order might very well be form—instrument—composer. This would mean that in a library arranged under the first order the books would appear on the shelves as follows: general studies—composers—forms—instruments; and in the second library: general studies—forms—instruments—composers.

Unfortunately books do not deal with single subjects such as 'Mozart', or 'pianos' or 'concertos', but are much more likely to deal with 'Mozart's piano concertos'. Any arrangement must allow for this and there are two ways of providing for these compound subjects. The traditional method is to be found in such schemes as the LC classification, which attempts to enumerate all the possible compound subjects. The modern method is found in the BCM classification, which provides the foci within the facets and rules on combining these foci to form compound subjects.

Thus for the first library mentioned above the traditional method would produce this sample order:

A1	Beethoven
A2	Haydn
A3	Mozart
A3.1	concertos
A3.11	piano
A3.2	symphonies
B1	fugues
B2	suites
B3	concertos
B3.1	piano

C1	violin
C2	cello
C3	piano

The book on Mozart's piano concertos would go at A3.11 and not at B3.1, because it has been decided that in this particular library composer was the most important aspect. Additionally a fundamental rule of all classification is that an item must be placed in the most specific head that will contain it. Nevertheless the traditional method does result occasionally in confusion and cross-classification if care is not exercised both in the construction of the scheme and in its application.

The modern method would provide the facets in a given order, listing the foci under each facet:

Composers
   1 Beethoven
   2 Haydn
   3 Mozart
Forms
   1 concertos
   2 symphonies
   3 fugues
Instruments
   1 piano
   2 cellos
   3 violas

The scheme would provide clear instructions on the order of combination of terms from these facets. In this example the combination order would be composers/forms/instruments. Thus the book must be analysed into Mozart/piano/concertos. These foci are then placed in their correct combination order Composer=Mozart/Form=concertos/Instrument=piano. The number for each focus is then taken from its appropriate facet and combined in order to give the final notation for the book as 311.

The advantage of the newer method is apparent immediately we have to classify a book on a compound subject which has not been catered for by the traditional scheme. For example, until recently Haydn was not generally considered as a composer of operas, but now there is great interest in this side of his activity. Because of the earlier neglect our traditional scheme would probably not have specified 'Haydn operas' and somehow a place would have to be made. The modern or faceted scheme would have provided

Composers
Haydn

20

Form
    operas

Therefore the compound subject can easily be formed by combining the two numbers in the correct order.

The main facets to be considered in the arrangement of music scores are composers, instruments, forms, size of ensemble. Other facets which may need to be considered are character, space, time. The same principles will apply here as in the arrangement of musical literature and the two methods of classification will be found in use in arranging scores.

Two further points need to be considered, however, in relation to the scores. The first is the frequency with which arrangements are met in music. It is one of the major problems of cataloguing music, but is it a problem in placing the material on the shelves? Here once again the answer must depend on the kind of library. A public library where most readers will want music for a particular instrument need not consider the problem. Flautists want music for the flute, whether originally scored or arranged for the instrument. A learned society's library on the other hand might well have to take account of arrangements and specify them under a composer, for example, further indicating the original instrumentation.

The second point is the very obvious division which needs to be made, in dealing with scores, between vocal and instrumental music. It would seem logical to extend this division to the literature. It is generally accepted that mixed vocal/instrumental scores are placed with the vocal group.

In this chapter the main concern has been to analyse the basic problems of organising material, by examining the kinds of approaches that readers make in music libraries and reducing the contents of books and scores to their basic elements. It can be seen that readers' needs are matched by these elements and therefore the problems can be solved very simply by individual librarians by making their primary arrangement equal the primary need of their readers. Unfortunately not all librarians have readers whose needs fall into one category. Therefore having decided on an order for the material on the shelves most suited to the needs of the majority of their readers, they must help others by supplementing that order by means of catalogues. Thus if an order for the shelves is used which gives priority to the instrument, the reader interested in music by a particular composer can be helped by means of a composer catalogue.

In attempting to help the reader interested in particular subjects within music such as harmony, acoustics, opera and film music, to find his material, the librarian can use a variety of methods. These will be discussed together with other problems specifically relating to cataloguing in the second volume.

To conclude, the following tabulated list of the facets revealed in music will be found useful in the following chapters where the major schemes are examined.

FACETS IN MUSIC

1 Facets in literature and music
   1 Composers (eg Verdi)
   2 Instruments (eg organ)
   3 Size of ensemble (eg quartet)
   4 Forms
      a) major (eg concertos)
      b) minor (eg binary)
2 Facets in literature and possibly in music
   5 Musical character (eg film music)
   6 Space (eg France)
   7 Time (eg baroque)
3 Facets in literature and unlikely in music
   8 Elements (eg harmony)
   9 Techniques (eg orchestration)
  10 Theory (eg appreciation)
  11 Forms of presentation (eg catalogues)
  12 Phase relationship (eg the architecture of concert halls.)

CHAPTER TWO

SPECIAL SCHEMES

THERE ARE of course many schemes for music which have been devised by librarians for their own libraries. It is impossible to look at all of these, but one of them at least (the Dickinson Classification) has been published and this will be examined; not perhaps as typical of them, because its compiler probably spent more time than most trying to perfect his scheme, but as an example along with the other classifications discussed in this chapter of the excellent work that has been done by music classificationists.

Some of the schemes dealt with in the next chapter, on general bibliographic classifications, could also count as special. In the case of the Library of Congress and McColvin schemes, for example, it is quite feasible to operate them independently of the general scheme of which they are designed to form a part. But they were after all designed primarily to operate in libraries using LC and DC respectively.

On the other hand the schemes in this chapter were all devised to operate independently. They are therefore special in that very limiting sense and merit special comment. Of these only BCM was constructed by a classificationist who was not also a music specialist. It is interesting, but perhaps not surprising, that this emerges as probably the best classification yet to be devised for music and music literature.

The BCM classification

The BCM first appeared in 1957 and its publication was one of the most important events in the history of music publishing. It is not necessary to discuss its bibliographical importance here, as we are concerned only with its possibilities as a classification scheme. It is not irrelevant to mention that music publishers, booksellers, and continental as well as British librarians have all paid tribute to its simplicity of use as a bibliography. In volume two an assessment is made of the effectiveness of the bibliography as a subject index.

The scheme was designed principally by E J Coates, at that time on the staff of BNB, in consultation with members of the United Kingdom branch of the International Association of Music Libraries. It is therefore an interesting example of collaboration between a classification specialist and people fully acquainted with the problems of attempting to organise the subject literature in libraries. It is important in the history of classification as the first *printed* fully faceted scheme published in Great Britain. It is based, therefore, on the principles of classification developed by Dr Ranganathan.

The literature of music is quite clearly separated from scores, and whenever possible the same notation is used for parallel subjects:

AS Books on the violin

S Scores for violin

Violin, the common factor here, is represented by S. The schedules provide places and notation for foci in various facets of music. The user of the scheme expresses the compound subjects in books and scores by combining the notational elements for the appropriate foci to produce a compound number. Thus:

WT=horn

E =sonata

Sonata for horn=WTE.

Following the principles considered in chapter one, the expected rule of procedure is provided for number building. The rule for this scheme can probably be understood if an outline of the structure is given.

Outline tables

A – BZ	LITERATURE OF MUSIC
A	General works
A(B) – A(WT)	Common subdivisions
A(X)	History of music
A(Y)	Music in particular localities
A(Z)	Music in relation to other subjects
A/AM	Theory
A/CY	Technique
A/FY	Musical character
A/LZ	Elements
A/S	Forms (ie binary, etc)
AB	Vocal music
AL	Instrumental music
B	Biographies and studies of composers
BZ	Non-European music

C – Z MUSIC – SCORES

CB	Vocal music
L	Instrumental music
Z	Non-European music

At the beginning of the section for SCORES under C an arrangement is provided for educational material consisting primarily of exercises not limited to a particular instrument, collected works of individual composers and collections of illustrative music. All of these symbols can be applied to symbols drawn from the vocal and instrumental classes. This will be demonstrated in examining the treatment of vocal music. Some examples of this type of material classed at the beginning of class C follow.

C/AC	Tutors
C/AZ	Collections from individual composers
C/G – C/L	Collections to illustrate music of a particular character
C/G	Folk music
C/H	Dance music
C/JR	Film music
C/L	Religious music
C/LZ	Collections illustrating the various elements of music
C/S	Collections illustrating the various forms

A slightly more detailed outline of the arrangement under class L INSTRUMENTAL MUSIC follows:

M	Orchestral music
MP	Solo instrument and orchestra
MT	Jazz
N	Chamber music
PW	Keyboard instruments
RW	String instruments
RX	Bowed
T	Plucked
U	Wind instruments

It can be seen from this that the arrangement is from large to small groups and that the instruments are arranged according to the method by which they are played. It is also apparent that the notation is not expressive.

Several auxiliary tables are provided. The first is the most important as it includes sub-arrangements for use under instruments and instrumental groups. This enables such facets as *form* and *size* to be expressed

25

simply. Certain parts of this table can be applied to orchestral and chamber music. Other tables are special subdivisions for keyboard instruments, ethnic or locality subdivisions (*space* facet) and chronological reference points (*time* facet).

There are two indexes, the first being to the table of ethnic or locaility subdivisions and the second a general subject index to the main tables. This index must never be used as a substitute for the tables in classifying. It is only an index to the elements which appear in the schedules and it does not include any compound subjects.

An examination of the outline table will show that the general or diffuse concepts in music come first (theory, techniques), while the more concrete come last (composers, instruments). The rule for forming compound numbers is simply: *Arrange elements of a title in reverse schedule order*. Apply this to the example 'Sonata for horn':

Schedule order:

E sonata

WT horn

Reverse schedule order:

horn/sonata

WTE

Therefore the order in expressing a compound subject is from the concrete to the diffuse, or from a thing to an idea.

Schedules:

idea:diffuse/general — concrete/thing

sonata   horn

Compound subject in a score or book:

concrete/thing — idea/diffuse/general

horn   sonata

In discussing order in chapter one a sample schedule was built up (page 20) in which the schedule order was the same as the order of the elements in a compound subject. The principle is exactly the same in the BCM scheme. All that has been done is to reverse the schedule order because usually it has been found that readers approach knowledge from the general to the particular. A simple example of this is the method of any study which usually proceeds in this way.

Students sometimes find difficulty in understanding this procedure, but anyone using this scheme need not worry, for the introduction explains the method and there are tables giving the main facets for both scores and literature, in the order in which each may contribute elements to the compound subjects.

26

For scores and parts:

EXECUTANT	FORM OF COMPOSITION	CHARACTER
piano	suite	Christmas

The EXECUTANT facet has the following sub-facets, expressed in this order:

1 *Vocal music*

SIZE OR COMPLEXITY	TYPE	ACCOMPANIMENT
duets	baritone	piano

2 *Instrumental music*

TYPE	SIZE	ACCOMPANIMENT	ORIGINAL EXECUTANT
flute	solo	none	oboe

For musical literature

COMPOSER	EXECUTANT	FORM	ELEMENTS	CHARACTER
Bach	organ	fugue	counterpoint	

TECHNIQUE	COMMON SUBDIVISION
sight reading	

The title chosen here is imaginary and unlikely, but it shows the use of these tables. With any title it is simply a matter of asking a number of questions in the correct order. Thus:

Sight reading Bach's counterpoint in his fugues for organ

QUESTION	ANSWER
1 Who is the *composer*?	1 Bach
2 What or who is the *executant*?	2 Organ
3 What is the *form*?	3 Fugue
4 What is the *element*?	4 Counterpoint
5 What is the *musical character*?	5 –
6 What is the *technique*?	6 Sight reading
7 What is the *common-subdivision*?	7 –

Having asked the questions, the classifier must then consult the schedules with the answers to build the correct number. The questions were asked in reverse schedule order, therefore the notational elements must combine in that way.

Terms in schedule order with notation:

6 Sight reading	A/EAG
4 Counterpoint	A/RM
3 Fugue	A/Y
2 Organ	AR
1 Bach	BBC

Instructions under B explain that, in adding symbols to a biography number, the initial A is retained when adding symbols from AB-AY, but

27

those drawn from A(A)–A/Z drop the initial A. Therefore taking the notational element for each answer in reverse schedule order, ie the order in which the questions were asked, gives the composite symbol:

BBCAR/Y/RM/EAG

This is a very long number, which draws attention to a criticism frequently made, namely, that the symbols in the *British catalogue of music* are too long. There are several points to make here:

1 This is an imaginary title, deliberately designed to introduce as many facets as possible.

2 The scheme is used as the basis of arrangement of a national bibliography. It is used as the filing medium in the main part of the bibliography and as a link between that part and the alphabetical index. Its length and accuracy enables an item to be placed very precisely and it also ensures that all concepts will be expressed in the index by isolating them in analysis.

3 Because this is a faceted scheme the classifier using the scheme in a library can modify it easily to suit his own purpose. The compound symbols are not supplied by the scheme, but constructed by the classifier. He need only use that part of the compound symbol co-extensive with the needs of his readers. In a given library situation this might be:

BBC AR/Y *Bach's organ fugues*

For indexing purposes he would be advised to work out the complete number, but index to the final limited symbol those terms expressed by elements beyond that part of the symbol selected:

Sight reading : Counterpoint : Fugues : Organ : Bach BBC AR/Y
and
Counterpoint : Fugues : Organ : Bach BBC AR/Y

This would ensure that the needs of the reader interested in those concepts would not be neglected.

Reference was made above to the use made in the bibliography of the classification as a filing medium. A feature here is the very broad base achieved by the use of three sets of symbols (A)–(Z), /A–/Z and A–Z. The arranging or filing order of these symbols is always: ( )/A–Z.

The advantage of this is that the basic terms are expressed by very simple numbers. As the notation makes no attempt to express the relationship between subjects, it is easy to accommodate new subjects whenever they may be required. This is demonstrated from PW KEYBOARD INSTRUMENTS:

Q   Piano
QR   Harpsichord

QS	Spinet
QSQ	Virginals
QT	Glockenspiel (keyed)
QY	Celeste

As the notation does not express relationship, a new instrument in this family can be accommodated at any convenient point, due regard being made to any possible clash with existing symbols. QP is used in auxiliary table 2 for *piano solos*, but QZ has not been used and by adopting that symbol a whole possible range of extensions is opened for any future instruments in the family. With an expressive notation attempting to show relationships this would not be such a simple exercise.

The brevity of the notation in comparison with the Decimal and Library of Congress classifications is shown by the following three common examples. (This seems a fairer method than by selection of esoteric titles which some critics have used):

	BCM	DC	LC
Sonata for oboe	VTE	788.7	M67
Concerto for clarinet and orchestra	MPVVF	785.686204	M1024
Missa solemnis — full score	EMDG	783.2254	M2010

These three examples are typical of the majority of scores with which a classifier has to contend. In all three the BCM notation is no more difficult than that of either DC or LC. Yet in each case all the concepts are expressed by BCM, but in the first, for example, LC does not express *sonata* while in DC oboe and cor anglais are classed at 788.7 and again *sonata* cannot be indicated.

With reference to the symbol DG for *Ordinary of the mass* it should be noted that in 1968 alterations to the schedules at class D (CHORAL MUSIC) were introduced as follows:

D	Choral music
DC	Religious choral music
DD	Oratorios
DE	Cantatas
DF	Liturgical music
DFF	Roman Rite
DG	Ordinary of the mass
DGK	Proper of the mass
DGKAV	Requiem masses
DGKB	Office
DGL	Other services
DTZ	Secular choral music
DX	Cantatas

29

This means that all religious choral music is classed under DC, which includes oratorios, cantatas and liturgial music. As can be seen, secular cantatas are classed at DX, again exemplifying the adaptability of the notation. The re-arrangement removes the necessity to distinguish between masses written for liturgical and those for concert performance. There is always a danger that in seeking detailed specificity the classificationist will exceed the bounds of practicality which the actual material being classified permits, or the user requires.

Another section where there has been some revision is class X (PERCUSSION INSTRUMENTS) which now has the following sequence:

XQ	Drum
XR	Timpani (kettle drum)
XRR	Side drum
XRU	Bass drum
XRV	Tambourine
XS	Bells
XSR	Church bells
XST	Tubular bells
XT	Glockenspiel
XTQT	Cymbals
XTQV	Gong
XTQW	Triangle
XTR	Dulcimer
XTU	Castanets
XV	Bones
XW	Rattle

One feature in which the BCM scheme does seem excessively detailed is in the lengths to which the notation is taken to express the original executant in an arrangement. A simple example is: Piano arrangement of Bizet's *Carmen*.

Q	Piano
QP	Solo (from auxiliary table 2)
K/	Arrangements (from auxiliary table 1)
CC	Opera

giving QPK/CC

This means that all arrangements for solo piano from opera file together and all arrangements from pieces for, say, clarinet come together; but is the pianist really interested in the original scoring to the extent that he requires to have all arrangements of marches from films classed together at QPK/MGM/JR?

MGM   Marches
M   Orchestral music
GM   Marches (from auxiliary table 1)
C/JR   Film music (the C is dropped in compound symbols).

It would seem suficient to separate arrangements from works originally scored for the particular instrument or combination as LC does. It should be pointed out that the introduction to BCM does allow that opinions on this point will differ, and suggests the expression of instrumental arrangements of vocal works and of reductions of works for solo instrument and orchestra for the same instrument with piano accompaniment.

Combinations of instruments are very easily indicated in BCM. Instructions are to be found under N CHAMBER MUSIC. Some examples follow:

Sonata for viola and piano (Entry is made under the later symbol where instruments belong to different families).

Viola SQ

Piano P (auxiliary table 1) Solo with piano or other keyboard accompaniment

Sonatas E

SQPE

Suite for violin and cello (Entry is made under the earlier symbol when instruments belong to the same family).

S   Violin
PL   Solos with second instrument other than keyboard
SR   Cello
G   Suites
SPLSRG

String quartet (Combinations of more than two limited to one family are entered under the family).

RX   Bowed string instruments
NS   Quartets
RXNS

Piano trio (Special symbols are provided under N for mixed family ensembles of more than two instruments).

NX   String and keyboard ensembles
NT   Trios
NXNT

Vocal music is dealt with in basically the same way as instrumental music. An outline of that section of the schedules gives:

CB	Vocal music
CC	Opera
D	Choral music
DC	Religious choral music
DW	Songs
E	Choral works with an accompaniment other than keyboard instrument
EZ	Unaccompanied choral works
F–HY	Choral works. Special voices
F	Female
FL	Soprano
J	Unison choral works
JN	Single voices in combination
K	Vocal solos

Some examples follow to demonstrate this part in use:

Messiah – vocal score. Class D is used for vocal scores with keyboard accompaniment.

DD	Oratorios

Messiah – full score. Full scores go under E, the accompaniment being shown by the appropriate symbol from the instrumental section. In the case of orchestral accompaniment this is actually provided in the schedules: EM.

DD	Oratorios
EMDD	

Christmas carols for unaccompanied male voices

C/LF	Christmas
DP	Carols
EZ	Unaccompanied choral works
G	Male voices

GEZDP/LF (Note: in adding symbols from C/ the C is dropped).

Examples of compound numbers for single voices are given in the schedules. It is impossible to give examples covering every combination, but those given in this chapter should demonstrate the great flexibility of this scheme.

The literature of the subject is handled in the same way, except that the composer facet comes first in any compound symbol where appropriate. This can be clearly seen in the imaginary Bach example given earlier (page 27).

The ethnic/locality subdivisions in auxiliary table 6 are very full for Commonwealth countries and the United States, but not developed at all for other countries. This seems a pity in the case of countries such as Austria and Italy with a great musical tradition. Surely Vienna and Salzburg are met more frequently in music literature than, say, Norfolk or Nebraska. This means that countries other than the United States and those of the Commonwealth in the Western European tradition would have to alter this part of the scheme to suit their own needs. Countries in the non-European tradition are treated more fully at BZ. Symbols taken from table 6 are introduced by (Y . . .). Thus *Church music in Great Britain* would be A/LD(YC) where A/LD is CHURCH MUSIC and C is BRITISH from table 6. They can be added directly to /AY to indicate a collection of music relating to a particular country. It is not proposed to discuss table 7 (chronological reference points) as it seems unlikely that any library would use it and it is not an essential part of the scheme.

Greater attention has been given to this scheme than to the others described in this chapter because it is the first major scheme to be produced by British librarians for music and it is an intrinsic part of the national bibliography of music. Any reader who wishes to study it further can do so by taking any issue of the *British catalogue of music* and comparing his compound numbers for any title with those provided by the bibliography. It is important to work from the facet orders provided by the introduction to the scheme and set out on page 27 of this book, as indeed it is in checking any of the examples given above.

It is always possible to criticise any work adversely and one or two such comments follow. In reading them it should be remembered that, in the present writer's opinion, this scheme remains the finest classification of music in print. It arranges the facets of music in an order which is convenient to the majority of users of most libraries, and for expressing compound subjects it provides a systematic approach which places both books and scores under the basic terms which are likely to be used by the majority of users. Most readers wanting a book on Mozart's piano concertos will surely have the composer primarily in mind and most instrumentalists wanting music will surely want the music for their instrument in the same place, not separated under form or composer. Both needs are met by the BCM scheme. Obviously some libraries will require a different arrangement, and an interesting view on this is provided by Maurice B Line in the article listed in the bibliography on page 100.

JAZZ is placed at AMT between LIGHT ORGHESTRAL MUSIC and CHAMBER MUSIC. The form *jazz* for a particular instrument can be expressed by HX from auxiliary table 1. Better treatment would be to place it at BX, which has not been used and comes conveniently between music of the European tradition and the non-European tradition at BZ. This seems a very suitable place for a developed classification of jazz to appear. This idea was suggested to me by my colleague Derek Langridge, who has developed the proposal in an article in *Brio* (spring 1967, vol 4 no 1, 2-6). The schedules are outlined below.

It would be interesting to know why A/D(M) was used for collective biography of composers. It seems more logical for this to appear at B before the biographies of individual composers. There are some curious gaps in the alphabetical list of composers at B, but presumably such omissions can be easily rectified. It is perhaps justifiable to specify some rather obscure English composers, but it seems odd to include Anton Diabelli and not Bohuslav Martinu, Ludwig Spohr, Johann Hummel and Karl von Dittersdorf.

It may seem unfortunate that vocal and full scores of such works as *Messiah* are separated at D and EM, but this is a convenient arrangement for the shelves as the format of each is so different from that of the other and in the bibliography they are brought together under the composer in the index.

Extension scheme for jazz, with examples of works appropriately classified.

BX   Jazz — general works
   Newton, Francis *The jazz scene*
BX(C) — Encyclopedias
   Panassie, H and Gautier, M *Dictionary of jazz*
BX(D) — Composite works
   Traill, S and Lascelles, G (eds) *Just jazz*
BX(L) — Social aspects
   Hentoff, N *The jazz life*
BX(T) — Bibliographies
   Merriam, A P *A bibliography of jazz*
BX(X) — History
   Hobson, W *American jazz music;* Stearns, M *The story of jazz*
BX(X/EM) — Illustrations
   Keepnews, O and Grauer, B *A pictorial history of jazz*
BX(Y) - Localities
BX(YAF) — New York
   Charters, S and Kunstadt, L *Jazz: a history of the New York scene*
BX(YC) — Great Britain
   Boulton, D *Jazz in Britain*

BX/C – Analysis

Hodeir, A *Jazz: its evolution and essence*; Ostransky, L *The anatomy of jazz*

BX/E – Performance

Traill, S (ed) *Play that music: a guide to playing jazz*

BX/FD – Recorded jazz

BX/FD(WT) – Discographies

Rust, B *Jazz records A–Z*

BX/FD/C – Appreciation

Fox, C et al *Jazz on record: a critical guide*

BX/LZ – Elements

Sargeant, W *Jazz: a history* (originally *Jazz: hot and hybrid*)

BX/Z – Styles

BX/ZM – Bebop

Feather, L *Inside bebop*

BXB – BXY – Instruments of jazz

BXWS – Trumpet

McCarthy, A *The trumpet in jazz*

BXZ – Jazz musicians – biography and criticism

Shapiro, N and Hentoff, N *The jazzmakers*

BXZ/ZM – Modern

James, M *Ten modern jazzmen*

BXZA – Louis Armstrong – biography and criticism

McCarthy, A *Louis Armstrong*

BXZA(P) – Biography

Armstrong, L *Satchmo: my life in New Orleans*

BXZA/FD(WT) – Discography

Jepsen, J G *A discography of Louis Armstrong*

BXZB – Count Basie

Horricks, R *Count Basie and his orchestra*

BY – Afro-American Music

BYA – Afro-American Music of the USA

Courlander, W H *Negro folk music USA*

BYC – Spirituals

Chambers, A *Treasury of Negro spirituals*

BYF – Blues

Oliver, P *Blues fell this morning*

BYF/FD(WT) – Discography

Dixon, R M W and Godrich, J *Blues and Gospel records 1902–1942*

BYFZ – Blues musicians
BYFZB(P) – Big Bill Broonzy - biography
    Broonzy, W *Big Bill Blues*
BYH – Ragtime
    Blesh, R and Janis, H *They all played ragtime*
BYJ – Jazz-tinged popular music
BYJZ - Musicians
BYJZC – Bing Crosby - biography and criticism
    Ulanov, B *The incredible Crosby*
BYJZC(P) – Biography
    Crosby, B *Call me Lucky*
BYJZC/FD(WT) – Discography
    Mello, E J and McBride, T *Bing Crosby: a discography 1926–1946*
BYK – BYZ – Afro-American traditions in other parts of America

The outline is based largely on compound numbers produced by combining **BX JAZZ** with foci from the main schedules:

The trumpet in jazz

AWS	Trumpet
BX	Jazz
BXWS	

Other elements have been produced by extending the existing schedules in an appropriate way:

Inside bebop

A/S	Forms of music
A/Y	Fugue
A/Z	Jazz styles
A/ZM	Bebop
BX	Jazz
BXZM	

Langridge does not claim this to be a perfect arrangement, but within the limitations of an existing scheme it is an effective and workable compromise. (See chapter four for a more detailed discussion on jazz).

The Dickinson Classification

This scheme, an American special scheme for music, was devised by George Sherman Dickinson for use in the Vassar College Library, Poughkeepsie, New York. It was originally published in 1938 as *Classification of musical compositions: a decimal–symbol system* and subsequently reprinted in *The Dickinson Classification: a cataloguing and classification manual for music* by Carol June Bradley (Carlisle, Pennsylvania,

Carlisle Books, 1968). The manual will be more fully discussed in volume two.

This scheme, as its title suggests, is intended for the classification of music only and not for the literature. It is, moreover, almost entirely limited to western classical music. It was intended primarily for the collection at the compiler's own library. It therefore makes no attempt to cover materials not in that library. It would be unfair therefore to apply the same critical standards to this scheme as those applied to the more general schemes in relation to its failure to cover, say, popular music. It is a most interesting scheme and has like LC the merit of immediate practical application to an existing collection, this time at the Vassar College Library. Dickinson was able to try his scheme out on the library's collection of scores and parts and thus to discover any faults before he actually published it.

It is incorrect to refer to the schedules of this scheme, as none are published. The scheme consists of a number of tables, each representing a category which might be thought necessary for the classification of a collection. Examples are:
Instrumental; Vocal; Species (eg sonatas, fugues, masses, vespers); Historical.

If a library opts to use the scheme, the librarian must decide on a combination order of the tables to provide an arrangement most suited to the needs of the library's users. This could involve the use either of all the tables or of a selected number. 'Once such selection has been made for a given situation, the system congeals for that particular library into a specific schedule, *which must be maintained to avoid confusion*. Rejected basic options are permanently eliminated, though the possibilities of decimal and symbol expansion under the actual options chosen remain open indefinitely. Expert judgment is therefore required in the original selection of options consonant with the character of a given library, though after the set-up is once determined classification may proceed in routine' (from the introduction to the original scheme).

Examples of various possible combinations are given in the introduction to the scheme. For a loan and performance library, material would be arranged primarily under the medium for which the music is arranged with the further possibilities of indicating the original medium, the composer, title and editor as part of the total call number. For reference and musicological libraries three choices are provided. All place the primary emphasis on the original medium, but vary in their arrangement of subsequent categories; one stresses the arrangement, the second the kind of score and the third the composer. The flexibility of the scheme is such that a library is not limited to the combinations suggested and demonstrated in the introduction, but can devise its own.

The scheme is thus a mixture of a faceted and an enumerative scheme. In a normal faceted scheme the facets are set out in citation order and foci are combined in accordance with the formula provided by the scheme each time an item is classified. In this scheme a library selects a combination order and then apparently proceeds to produce by synthesis an enumerative scheme for its own use. There would seem to be no reason why a library should not decide to operate the scheme as a normal faceted one, combining elements (foci) from categories (facets) each time an item is classified. The one essential feature of any method of operation is that once a combination order (citation order) has been decided on it must be adhered to rigidly throughout.

It is a very ingenious scheme. Its presentation is rather complicated and might put off potential users. Nevertheless careful reading of the instructions and examination of the tables, together with analysis of the worked examples, will bring full understanding of how the system operates.

Each table has an index letter which is never used in the classification symbol for an item, but is provided for ease of reference in using the scheme. The index letter in most cases is the initial letter of the name of the table.

L   location
g   grouping
S   species

The tables are not arranged in alphabetical order, but an alphabetical index of index letters is provided at the front.

The ultimate purpose of the system is to produce a call number from the tables. Such a number making maximum use of the tables would be likely to have elements representing *location, classification* (medium), *extension* (eg original medium, accompaniment), *distinction* (eg composer, title, editor).

The notation employs numerals, used decimally except those in (   ), symbols and letters.

Examples of the symbols are:

O   accompaniment
=   arranged
/   excerpt, eg opus 76 no 1 is (76/1)
♭♮♯   key

38

The tables with examples of elements contained in them are grouped under the headings listed above.

1 *Location* Under (L) there are terms representing the placing of materials:

M Music (only used when music library is a department of a larger library)

p Parts

t Treasure room or locked cases.

2 *Classification* Here the main class *medium of performance* (CD B) appears:

1 Keyboard solo

2 String (bowed) solo

3 Wind solo

4 Plectral solo and other

46 Percussion

5 Chamber ensemble

52 String (bowed)

6 Orchestral

7 Voice solo and solo ensemble

8 Choral

9 Dramatic

91 Opera

It is preceded by a miscellaneous class representing forms of publication:

01 Manuscripts

04 Monuments

07 Tutors

and followed by (1) *Species* (S) which provides a list of terms by which the appropriate divisions can be divided:

1 *Sonatas* (when applied to instruments), *Songs* (when applied to vocal solos, secular or sacred), *Oratorios* (when applied to choral works).

3 *Overtures* (when applied to orchestras), *Cycles* (when applied to vocal solos) etc.

(2) *Historical categories* (H) which can be developed by individual libraries if needed for eg subdivision 19 *obsolete keyboard* and similar divisions under other classes.

3 *Extension* Here comes

I Medium

 a Accompaniment

  01 keyboard

  06 orchestral

       v   Voices
            — m   men's voices
            — w   women's voices
       g   Grouping
            — 2   duo
            — 3   trio
       t   Tessitura
            — h   high voice
            — 1   low voice
  II   Form
       F   Arranged for or from
            = 1   keyboard
            = 6   orchestral
       Fa   Arranged for, accompaniment only
            = 01   keyboard
            = 03   wind
  III Qualification
       n   Nationality
             [F4] Finnish
             [F8] French
       r   Religion
             [A6] Anglican
             [J5] Jewish
       d   Date
             ( )   century
             ( )   year
       O   Occasion
             1   New Year
             2   Lent
             8   liturgic
             9   patriotic
4 *Distribution*
  1   *Book mark* (B) which comprises a compiler mark for collections
      or composer mark for individual composer's work
  2   *Title mark* (T)
  3   *Edition mark* (E) for editor and edition number.
It will have been noted that there is a strong mnemonic feature in the
notation eg *Keyboard* is always represented by 1 and *Orchestral* by 6.
Mnemonic features are sometimes of doubtful value, because it is difficult
to apply them throughout in the reverse process ie 1 does not always

mean *keyboard*. Nevertheless it seems to work well with this scheme, as it is nearly always possible to tell by the context when 1 means keyboard, once familiarity with the notation has been achieved.

It is possible to express all the standard required concepts for music scores. Some examples follow to demonstrate the schemes application in a performance collection:

String quartet (parts) p 52 − 4 or 52 − 4
                                           p

p	Parts (This comes first if parts are filed separately)
52	String (bowed) from table CD B
−4	Quartet from table g
p52 − 4	(parts filed separately)

52 − 4
p   (parts not filed separately).

Piano arrangement of a symphony 111=6

11	Piano solo from table CD B
1	Symphony from table S
=6	Arranged from Orchestra, from table F.
111=6	(Note that the *form* in this case subdivides the instrument for which arranged, not the original. This seems quite logical).

Christmas carols for unaccompanied male choir

8	Choral from Table CD B
00	Unaccompanied from Table a
−m	male from Table v
6	Occasional from Table S
.6	Christmas from Table 0

800 − m 6.6.

The symbols for location are added below these main class numbers by the use of Cutter numbers for composers, arrangers, etc,initial letters for titles of works and editors eg

L 69	Liszt
p K	(Les) Préludes ed by Klauser

If the first example above referred to Beethoven's *String quartet op 18 no 1* this could be fully expressed as

p52 − 4	
B39	Beethoven
(18/1)	Op 18 no 1

The notes to the original scheme contain many examples to demonstrate how the scheme works. Further, the manual in the 1968 publication contains the cataloguing manual and classification charts in use at the

State University of New York and at Vassar for collections where the primary emphasis is on study rather than performance. These show the full implementation of the scheme and give further examples.

Within its limitations of western classical music, this is an admirable scheme which deserves more serious attention in this country than it has yet received. In particular it would be very useful for college music libraries, where the emphasis is on performance, while the schedules demonstrated in the manual would be excellent as the basis for a study collection.

German special schemes

In a paper read at the IAML Conference at Cambridge in 1959 Dr Alfons Ott suggested a very simple classification for scores which small libraries might find useful (*Music libraries and instruments* London, Hinrichsen, 1961, 79—83). In this, instrumental music is divided to provide places for scores according to the quantity a small library is likely to have. Thus, piano music is divided into solo, duet and two pianos, while wind music is divided only into woodwind, brass, recorder and chamber music in which wind features. Orchestral music is divided simply into full and miniature scores. This scheme is commended for its simplicity to librarians who have only a small collection.

The arrangement for vocal music is shown in full:

II VOCAL MUSIC

1   Songs with piano accompaniment
2   Songs with accompaniment other than piano
3   Choral music:
    a unaccompanied children's and female voices
    b unaccompanied male voices
    c unaccompanied mixed voices
    d voices with instrumental accompaniment
4   Vocal scores:
    a operas and operettas
    b oratorios and other sacred and secular choral works

SMM scheme

This German scheme: *Systematik der Musikliteratur und der Musikalien für öffentliche Musikbüchereien* (Reutlingen, Verlag Bücherei und Bildung, 1963) was prepared by the West German national Branch of IAML and was obviously influenced by Dr Ott's scheme. It can be seen in use in *Musikbibliographischer Dienst*, the excellent German bibliographical service for music.

Unlike Dr Ott's scheme it has not been translated into English. As its title suggests it is intended for the classification of music literature and scores in public libraries. It is larger than the Ott scheme and in scope is comparable with the McColvin scheme, the simplicity of its structure being reminiscent of that of the latter. It is mentioned here for the sake of completeness, but it is unlikely to receive much attention in the English speaking world as so many native schemes already exist and the German one, useful as it is, does not add anything particularly distinctive, although there are interesting alternative arrangements to those in McColvin, one of which is exemplified below. Dr Ott's scheme on the other hand might serve very well for a small public library with the kind of collection he suggests.

It is interesting to compare SMM and McColvin in their arrangement of chamber music.

SMM		McColvin	
H	Music for wind	782.1	Duets and trios for strings
K	Chamber music for wind	.2	Trios for piano and strings
L	Music for strings	.3	Quartets for strings
M	Chamber music for strings	.4	Quartets for piano and strings
N	Chamber music for strings and other instruments without piano	.5	Quintets, sextets etc for strings, piano and strings
O	Chamber music for piano	.6	Chamber music incl wind instruments

Within each class SMM subdivides by size of group, so the arrangement is exactly the reverse of that in McColvin. The German scheme brings together the music for individual instruments within a family and the chamber music for that family, as for wind in classes H and K, which is an advantage as players are likely to find such an arrangement useful. On the other hand players may be able to use music for other instruments within the same size of group; their search is then made fractionally easier by McColvin, although his primary principle of division by size does not apply to the separation of music for wind instruments at 782.6. The German scheme uses numerals for further division.

Ivan Pethes's draft scheme

Mention must also be made of *A flexible classification system of music and literature on music*, compiled by Ivan Pethes (Budapest, Centre of Library Science and Methodology, 1967). This is a draft scheme

43

devised by its compiler for discussion by the IAML Classification Sub-commission. It is an interesting attempt to adapt the principles of UDC to a fully faceted approach. It is needless to say a considerable improvement on the UDC schedules. Its ouline follows:

0	MUSICOLOGY, LITERATURE
01	Scientific basis
02	Theory
03	Composition and performance
04	Persons in music
05	Organisations
06	Phase relationships
07	History
08	Folk music
09	Reference books
1/9	MUSIC
11	Woodwind
12	Brass
14/16	Strings
14	Bowed
15	Plucked
16	Keyboard
17	Reed organs
171	Organ
18	Percussion
19	Electronic
2	Chamber music
22	Two instruments
24	Four instruments
29	Nine instruments
3	Orchestral music
4	Soloist with ensemble/orchestra
5	Vocal music: solo voice
51	Undefined voice
52	Children
53	Female
54	Male
55/58	Solo voice with accompaniment divided as 51/54
6	Vocal ensemble
64	Quartet with instruments
68	Octet with instruments

7	Choral
8	Soloists, choirs and orchestras
9	Collected editions

In addition to these main tables a series of auxiliary tables are provided:

−1/−4	Historical periods
−5	Form of instrumental composition
−6	Vocal forms
−7	Form of theatre music
−8	Schools, transcription
−9	The outward appearance of compositions

Full use is made of the UDC connecting symbols and in the examples given in the draft some very long numbers result:

Requiem for tenor solo, children's choir and mixed choir and full orchestra

8	Compositions for singers, choir and symphony orchestra
582	Tenor solo accompanied
78	Children's and mixed choir
39	Symphony orchestra
−614	Requiem

858.2' 78' 39 − 614

Like UDC the scheme would permit various citation orders:

Piano sonata

Piano 161
Sonata −511
either 161 − 511 or 1 − 511 : 161, where 1=instrumental music.

There is some attempt to deal with other forms of music, so under each division of music scores provision is made for folk music:

115	Oboe
115.6	Folk type oboes
14	Bowed string
146	Other friction instruments

As can be seen from the placing of piano music under strings some account has been taken of the work of ethnomusicologists. In fact the arrangement of piano and organ is a nice compromise between the ethnomusicologists' demand for a division by acoustical principles and the needs of the classical musician. Objection can immediately be made to the placing of organ under reed organ.

The treatment of jazz is very odd. It appears at −67 as a subdivision of Vocal forms of music and at 314 under Compositions for dance orchestra.

Like any synthetic scheme it could be used at any level of synthesis and with some tidying up could very well replace the full UDC schedules, but it lacks the neatness of BCM as a faceted scheme. It has formed the basis of much useful discussion and at times fierce argument in subsequent meetings of the Classification Subcommission at IAML Conferences. Some account of these is given in the brief reports which appear regularly in *Fontes artis musicae*. Further reference to the work of the subcommission will be made in the second volume of this book.

Classification according to musicological scheme

It is the practice of some libraries, particularly on the continent, to arrange their collections according to the systematic arrangement used in some of the standard bibliographies of music. It is not proposed to deal at any length with these schemes, as this method is unlikely to be used in this country where the majority of librarians seem to prefer a scheme devised by a classificationist rather than one developed by a musicologist. As the latters' schemes seem to differ from each other as frequently as do the formers', the librarian is as likely to find difficulty with one of these schemes as he is with one of the traditionally acceptable classifications.

For the classified index to its *Chamber music catalogue* the British Broadcasting Corporation used a modified form of the classification devised by Wilhelm Altmann for his *Kammermusik-Katalog*; it may be convenient therefore to examine this arrangement as typical of those offered by the bibliographies of music, further details of which are provided in the bibliography on page 101. There is no notation, but one could easily be provided if required.

Group I is CHAMBER MUSIC WITHOUT KEYBOARD. This is arranged by size of ensemble from septets, octets etc, to duos. Each size is subdivided into strings, strings and wind, wind. From quintets downwards the division is more precise, allowing under quintets, for example, for two violins, two violas, cello *or* two violins, viola, two cellos, and under quartets for four violins, four violas or four cellos as well as the more usual combinations.

Group II is CHAMBER MUSIC WITH KEYBOARD, which employs very nearly the same principles of division allowing for the different kinds of ensemble met in this group. Thus under trios:

keyboard, violin, viola
keyboard, violin, cello
keyboard, two violins

keyboard, two cellos
keyboard, string, wind
keyboard, wind
keyboard, miscellaneous.

Under duos comes the very large number of sonatas for keyboard and other instruments, although sonata is not specified in the classification.

Group III is VOICES WITHOUT KEYBOARD. Once again basic division is by size:

two or more voices with various accompaniment
voice with string quartet
voice with three strings or wind
voice with two strings or wind
voice with single string or wind

Group IV is VOICE WITH KEYBOARD, very similarly arranged.

Group V SELECTED INSTRUMENTS WITH ACCOMPANIMENT is rather curiously named as it includes guitar and harp solos as well as such divisions as harp and clarinet, percussion with instruments and baryton trios (viz those by Haydn). The principle of selection is not explained, but this group seems to include solo music for those instruments not normally found in a symphony orchestra as well as other music for those which are; although this principle seems false when Group VI, SELECTED SOLO INSTRUMENTS, while including the normal instruments of a symphony orchestra, includes bagpipe, coach-horn and regal.

The BBC Music Library is one of the finest collections of music in the world and has probably been used by most of the world's greatest musicians. Its choice of a classification must therefore be founded on considerable practical experience. This scheme based on Altmann does seem good in its broad outline and in its use of the *size* facet as a primary means of division, but it becomes very muddled in its last two groups, as has been shown. In fact it would surely be simpler to have one group only for solo instrument and to place such items as Haydn's baryton trios under trios, which is where they logically belong in a scheme arranged by size.

CHAPTER THREE

TREATMENT OF MUSIC
IN SOME GENERAL SCHEMES OF CLASSIFICATION

CLASSIFICATIONISTS SUCH AS Melvil Dewey, James Duff Brown and
Henry Evelyn Bliss face an almost impossible task in attempting to organise the whole of knowledge. There has been a great deal of discussion
among philosophers about the ideal order in which to systematise man's
collective wisdom. An examination of the best known general schemes
reveals some interesting close relationships for music:

DC		BC		LC	
600	Technology	U	Useful arts	L	Education
700	Fine arts	V	Aesthetic arts	M	Music
770	Photography	VR	Photography	N	Fine arts
780	Music	VU	Textile arts	P	Language and Literature
790	Recreation	VV	Music		
800	Literature	W	Philology		

	Brown		Colon	
C	Physical science	N	Fine arts
C300	Acoustics	NQ	Painting
C315	Sound recording	NR	Music
C400/700	Music	0	Literature
C800	Astronomy		

UDC has the same basic order as DC.

There is a measure of agreement here between most of the major schemes,
which place music in fairly close relationship to the fine arts and language
and literature. Only LC juxtaposes it to education. Brown's Subject Classification provides the most interesting placing and perhaps the most logical.
He objected to the categories fine and useful arts, developed a theory of
one place one subject, and placed activities which are usually a part of
fine or useful arts either in his Generalia class or immediately after the
physical science from which they stemmed. Hence music's close association with acoustics. Musicians wanting books on general acoustics rather

than musical acoustics have to go to another section of the library (eg class 534 in DC and class QC in LC) where other schemes are used. It is a matter for investigation perhaps as to what musicians would most welcome as a neighbouring class in a general library. Probably many have no particular need outside music when using the music library. If they have one it is likely to be acoustics, which, as Brown allows, is closely associated.

In examining the schedules for music itself in the general schemes, allowance has to be made for the fact that music is then only one among many classes; indeed in schems like DC and BC it is a division of a main class. This will affect the usefulness of the scheme for a special collection, in that for some classifying it will be necessary to consult the common subdivisions or categorical tables. This means that the whole scheme has to be purchased. Usually the notation will be longer than that of a special scheme, as the general scheme has to have a symbol representing music in order to separate it from the other classes.

Although this is not the fault of the scheme, it can also mean that music is classified in large libraries by general cataloguers/classifiers who place items incorrectly through a lack of understanding of the nature of the scores they are handling. Sometimes the music librarian may have little control over library policy on the processing of materials, but it may be an advantage if a specialist scheme is used. Observation of libraries seems to suggest that where special schemes are used the music librarian is more likely to have responsibility for processing material. However, the majority of libraries use one of the major schemes and it is interesting to examine their treatment of music. LC is examined first because of its special nature.

Library of Congress

This is a very important classification of music. It is not so modern in construction as BCM but it is intended for use in large libraries and was developed out of the experience gained in organising one of the largest and finest collections of music in the world. It is, therefore, an extremely practical scheme and any adverse criticism must be tempered by the knowledge that the Library of Congress provides a fine service to musicians and scholars throughout the world.

It is a part (class M) of the complete Library of Congress classification, which has been constructed empirically since the beginning of this century. There is much to be said for the method used, which was to base the classification upon a convenient arrangement of the books in the collection. Class M was published in 1904 and, like all the other main classes in the scheme, is complete in itself. LC is therefore a number of special subject schemes grouped together to form a general classification. This has the obvious advantage for a special library that individual parts can be purchased comparatively cheaply.

In the introduction, O G Sonneck, chief of the music division in 1904, stated that the scheme was based somewhat on the form of classified catalogue used by music publishers in arranging scores, and therefore appears somewhat different from the style favoured by librarians. This is really only a minor difference. It certainly does not prevent use of the scheme in libraries.

The schedules are divided into three main groups: M MUSIC; ML MUSIC LITERATURE; and MT MUSIC INSTRUCTION AND STUDY.

There is a combined relative index to all three sections at the back. It is important to realise that the schedules are constantly being revised in the light of experience. The tables are frequently reprinted and amendments, with their own index, are listed at the back of the volume after the general index. The amendments, which between each reprint are also listed in LC *Classification—additions and changes*, are not so drastic as to necessitate considerable reorganisation and are often helpful solutions to current problems.

A list of definitions appears at the beginning of M. These should be read carefully as a number of terms are used in the scheme in a special way.

'String instruments' are defined as string instruments with a bow. Compare BCM where this group is subdivided into bowed and plucked. For the latter, LC used 'Plectral instruments'. 'Early music' is used for music published or manuscript before 1800.

It follows that in the schedules, the period division for published works depends on the date of publication, not of composition. It is interesting to not that in the preface to a revised edition issued in 1917, Sonneck felt that a completely separate arrangement for early music would have been better, since it does involve special problems such as the precise difference between vocal and instrumental music and between chamber and orchestral music.

The order in MUSIC (class M) is:

M1 – M4 Collections—with special places for *Monuments of music* (ie Denkmäler) and collected editions of individual composers with special recognition of the significance of the Breitkopf and Härtel Gesamtausgaben.

M5 – M1459 Instrumental music–subdivided by size, divided by instrument. Orchestral music is arranged at M1000 – M1360.

M1490 Music (instrumental or vocal), printed or manuscript, before 1700 and preferred here, arranged by composers instead of assigned to special classes.

M1495 – M2197 Vocal music–subdivided secular (M1497 – M1998) and sacred (M1999 – M2199).

Under instrumental music, as has been stated, the basic division is by size. The instruments under solo are arranged in the order: keyboard - string - wind - plectral - percussion. Within each instrumental group the order, where appropriate, is the same as that found in most full scores (eg flute – oboe – clarinet etc). Piano and organ are subdivided by form:

M20 - 39 Piano music

M23 Piano sonatas

Other instruments are divided into miscellaneous collections; original compositions; arrangement.

Under some instruments (eg violin but not flute) a place is provided for simplified editions, and it would be interesting to know how the choice was made. It is difficult to believe that the Library of Congress has no simplified editions for the flute. Arrangements are entered under the instrument for which the piece has been arranged.

Duos involving a piano are all entered under piano. This means that Brahms's *Sonatas for clarinet and piano* will be entered at M250 under duos for piano and clarinet and not at M72 under clarinet, as might be expected by most clarinet players.

Orchestral music is subdivided first by type of orchestra and then by form:

M1000 – M1075 Symphony orchestra

M1001 Symphonies

M1004 Overtures, including opera overtures if detached (no specific place provided for these by BCM)

M1005 – M1041 Concertos–divided by solo instrument.

M1100 – M1160 String orchestra.

It is apparent from this that the order of applying facets in placing a composite score is: size of instrumental group/instrument/original composition or arrangement/form (for some instruments only).

Secular vocal music is arranged similarly by the size of the group, although while instrumental music proceeds from solo to orchestra, this starts with operas and finishes at solo songs:

M1500	— M1529 Dramatic music
M1500	Operas — full scores
M1502	Vocal scores - unaccompanied
M1503	Vocal scores — piano accompaniment
M1530	— M1546 Choral music — secular cantatas etc. Arranged — mixed, men's, women's, children's voices.
M1547	— M1610 Choruses and part-songs, not originally intended for orchestral accompaniment as at M1530 — M1546. Arranged — as M1530 — M1546.
M1611	— M1998 Songs, with a very detailed arrangment at the end of national songs arranged by country. Sacred vocal music is arranged differently. Form is used as the basic characteristic:
M2000	— M2007 Oratorios
M2010	— M2017 Masses
M2018	— M2036 Cantatas etc

Under M2079 (chorus, anthems, part-songs) there is a very full arrangement for settings of special texts in Latin and in English.

At M2147 — M2188 very full treatment is available for liturgies. This is for music only. The texts go in class B (religion).

The method of working, therefore, in classifying a vocal music score would be: secular or sacred (ie musical character) /form (in which size is implied by the order) /kind of voice (in most cases) /accompaniment.

MUSIC LITERATURE (ML) is arranged so that, as would be expected, general works come first, with librettos at ML48 — ML54. History and criticism forms a very large class (ML159 — ML3795). General histories come first, arranged by period, then the history of music in individual countries which are subdivided by use of a 'period table' at ML197.

Biography of individual composers is placed at ML410. This would also include criticism, although analytical guides appear at MT90 — MT150. There is an exceptionally detailed subdivision provided for Wagner, which it is claimed can be adapted for other prolific composers. It would not be easy to adapt however, and it would seem more sensible to make a special arrangement for each composer when required, although, as the scheme suggests, subdivision to any great detail under composers is probably best avoided.

There follows a somewhat haphazard and incomplete grouping of the two facets analysed in chapter one as *elements* (rhythm, melody etc) and *techniques* (instrumentation) with *forms* (general) in the middle:

ML 446   Counterpoint
ML 448   Forms (general)
ML 457   Conducting

There is no indication on how a book on the problems of conducting counterpoint should be classed; presumably, as the scheme goes from general to specific, under ML457. This is dealt with below.

The *instrument* facet comes next, arranged in the same order as in M, followed by sections for chamber and orchestral music. Both these categories of music and the individual instruments are subdivided by period and country. Books on vocal music follow, arranged similarly to the scores in M with country and period divisions where appropriate. Next ML has a grouping by country of books on national music (ML3545 – ML3775), where a careful distinction must be made between this and the history of music in general in a particular country (ML200). The final main division in ML is:

ML3800 – ML3920 Philosophy and physics of music.

Here go all the books on such subjects as acoustics, physiology, aesthetics and ethics when they are related to music. This type of subject would usually be better placed in the general works section at the beginning of ML, but it may have been placed here because it is obviously closely linked to MT.

MUSIC INSTRUCTION (MT) is a quite useful separation of books concerned with the teaching of different techniques in music, and particularly those devoted to individual instruments and the voice. The instruments are arranged in the same order as they are at M with subdivision under each instrument for general observations, systems and methods, studies and exercises – general, orchestral, self-instructors.

At MT90 (analytical guides) there is a special arrangement for Wagner again. A note at MT90 explains that this symbol is used for books on how to listen to and how to understand certain musical compositions. The more general studies will be placed at ML410. It is always possible to ignore MT90 and use ML410 for all books on a composer.

It is not easy to see the basic arrangement of either ML or MT in such a way that a book dealing with a compound subject can be classified with certainty. In fact it would probably be unfair to work out a facet order for compound subjects on the basis of the scheme. It would be safer for a classifier, working in a library and using this scheme, to compile his own facet order and apply it in all cases in order to achieve uniformity in placing books. To do this he would need to employ the techniques outlined in chapter one.

As it stands, the scheme is too detailed for most libraries, but the compilers give full permission in the preface to the revised edition (1917) for any convenient modification to be carried out. There is always the danger of cross-classification in schemes of the traditional type such as this, and some contraction of the schedules might reduce this risk. It is probably, too, that modern composers have written for combinations not covered in the LC schedules.

Jazz originated in the United States, but was of no special significance when the scheme appeared, nor even by 1917. It has had to be inserted since then and will be found only in the 'additions' at the back, where it is placed, under ML3551 United States, in the broad division national music, at ML3561. It has some odd companions, such as (also at 3561) A history of campaign songs, and ML3562 Festivals of civic patriotism.

This illustrates very clearly the difficulties of coping with new subjects in an enumerative scheme such as LC.

The Dewey Decimal Classification (18th edition)

This is the most widely used scheme in the English-speaking world, and can be seen in use in most American and British public libraries. It is a pity therefore that it is the least satisfactory of all the schemes in its treatment of music. Its extensive use means that of all the schemes it has been the most subject to practical criticism; it is possible that other schemes given the same intensive use for a hundred years would reveal as many faults.

Because of so many large libraries now using DC there is a great burden of feeling against change, even in the way the schedules of the scheme are revised to take account of modern knowledge and classification theory. This means that a reader using a number of libraries, all classified by Dewey, may well find that each uses a different edition of the schedules. This may have been modified in varying ways in the light of practical experience. Some changes in subsequent editions may also have been observed without complete acceptance of these editions. DC is an enumerative scheme and it is always more difficult to revise such schemes satisfactorily than it is to revise faceted schemes, which are much more easily manipulated because of their analytical and flexible approach to knowledge.

Comment on the sixteenth and seventeenth edition of DC will be found in the first edition of this book. The current edition of DC is the eighteenth, which attempts to take greater account of the principles of faceted classification by the introduction of a separate volume of tables, which can either be applied throughout the main schedules or to particular classes to produce compound numbers. In practice this has merely brought together in the separate volume operations previously subsumed in the main schedules or treated as common subdivisions, and can at the most be counted as a tidying up process. It can in no way be called a faceted scheme. However, a research team at the School of Librarianship, Leeds Polytechnic, has produced a completely revised schedule (known in DC as a 'Phoenix' schedule) for class 780 Music at the request of the DC Editorial Policy Committee; this is a faceted scheme based substantially on the work of Eric Coates for BCM and there is some hope that this might be included in the twentieth edition of DC. Comment on the Phoenix schedules follows that on the eighteenth edition.

The most obvious fault in the treatment of music in DC is perpetuated from edition to edition and remains still in this latest, the eighteenth. It is the failure to recognise the fundamental difference between the physical nature of books and of music with, consequently, no allowance made for such a difference in the scheme such as exists in LC, BC and BCM. The most it does is to provide a separate number for each within the same division:

787.1	Literature on the violin
787.15	Music for the violin

There is also an option that M can precede a number for a score. Yet, curiously, bibliographies of books about music are preferred at 016.78 or, following the alternative offered at 016, at 780.16 using 016 from table 1, while bibliographies of music are classed either at 016.78 for preference or at 781.97. It would seem useful to have all bibliographies of the subject in one place, especially as many cover both books and music. This can of course be achieved by using 016. A library limited to music might well prefer to use 780.16 for all kinds of bibliography.

780 covers general topics and has a useful feature at

780.81	Collected scores and parts by single composers
.82	The same by more than one composer
.84	Miniature scores, regardless of medium or kind

No indication is given of sub-arrangement here, but presumably 81 and 84 would be A–Z by composer. At least this grouping recognises the different physical forms of these kinds of score and the practical usefulness of having them so arranged.

781 General principles and considerations remains a hotch-potch. Given that students are instructed to check their classification in practical exercises to see if the item placed at a subdivision fits into the main class, of which the subdivision forms a part, how can Ragtime at 781.572

be said to be a part of 781 General principles and considerations? There appears also to be little in the way of logic about this sequence

781.67	Embellishment
.7	Music of ethnic and national orientation
.91	Musical instruments
.96	Words to be sung or recited with music

Apart from a few subdivisions under .7, which are concerned primarily with folk music, there is no other term in the schedules at this point than those listed above (.8 is not used).

782 Dramatic music. One useful aspect of DC's arrangement of books and music is that the librettos are arranged here with the scores.

783 Sacred music. Preference is for scores to be classed here as well as treatises, but the option to class scores and parts at 784 is available.

784 Voice and vocal music. Again literature and music are classed together, but perhaps a more serious criticism here is that 784 would appear to be the main division under which 782 and 783 should be subsumed. There are several possibilities of cross-classification in 784 between 784.3 where division is by size of group, 784.4 – 7 character by kind of group and 784.8 again by size but for items too general to be included in the earlier section. Further 784.4 is for Folk songs, but at 781.7 appears the quite clear instruction 'class folk music here'.

785 Instrumental ensembles and their music. At the beginning of this division a limited list is given of common subdivisions to be applied as specified within 785. Thus 785.12 Band music can be further subdivided to give, for example, 785.1206 Organisations connected with band music. At 785.0672 appears Jazz band, which can be subdivided to give Study and teaching 785.067207, which also appears at 781.57 Jazz and related forms. The music for symphony orchestra is scattered as in earlier editions:

785.1	Symphonies and band music
.11	Symphonies for orchestra
.12	Band music
.13	Military band music
.2	Music for orchestra with incidental vocal parts
.3	Miscellaneous music for orchestra
.32	Symphonic poems
.34	Variations
.4	Music for small ensembles
.42	Jazz
.5	Independent overtures for orchestra
.6	Concertos

.7	Chamber music	
.8	Suites for orchestra	

This is a quite astonishing sequence which seems to lack any logic.

A simpler approach would be to re-arrange the class completely to subdivide first by *kind* of ensemble and then by form:

785.1	Orchestras and their music	
.11	Symphonies	
.12	Symphonic poems	
.13	Variations	
.14	Suites	
.15	Concertos	
785.2	Bands	
.21	Symphonies	
.22/3	Variations	
.26	Dance music	
.27	Jazz	

etc.

Under 785.7 provision is made for the application of the size facet when instruments from different families are involved:

785.72 Duets. Add the number following 78 in 786 − 789, observing the table of precedence under 784 − 789, eg duets for flute and piano 785.72851 (flute is earlier in the table of precedence; its number is 788.51).

786 − 789 Instrumental music. Comprehensive works on musical instruments go at 781.91, which seems an unfortunate separation. Only under piano and organ is it possible to express form. When two or more instruments of the same kind are involved entry is made under the instrument and not under 785.7, thus music for three clarinets 788.62543. The facet order for scores is instrument, subdivided by size or form. It does not seem to be possible to subdivide by both.

Phoenix 780

This proposed new schedule for DC 780 is a remarkable achievement by Russell Sweeney, principal lecturer, and John Clews, research assistant, at Leeds Polytechnic. It was completed in draft form in 1975 and succeeds in introducing the basic structure of the BCM faceted scheme into the DC enumerative schedules without too great a wrench. In order to separate music scores from music literature it makes the option of using M to distinguish scores a compulsory aspect of the scheme. This and the re-arrangement of the schedules to make the composer the primary facet of the literature are perhaps the fundamental changes.

For music literature the citation order is composer — executant — form — character — techniques — elements — standard subdivisions. For scores the citation order is executant — form — character. In order to adjust the essentially hierarchical enumerative basis of the original schedule and its related notation to the new faceted order 1 has been used in addition to 0 and the 'divide like' principles, which are already used in DC, to introduce a new characteristic of division.

781.248	Themes
782.23	Oratorios
782.231248	Oratorio themes

It will be noticed that in combining these numbers only the essential element to express 'themes' has been taken from 781.248. The 1 is the indicator and not the 1 in 781.

The proposed outline schedules for the new 780 are:

780	Philosophy and theory
781	General principles
781.2	Elements
781.3	Composition
781.4	Techniques
781.5	Music for specific times, settings and media
781.6	Specific kinds of music
781.7	Forms
782—3	Voices and their music
784—8	Instruments and their music
789	Composers and other traditions of music

It can be seen from this that the schedule order is substantially the same as that found in BCM. In combining numbers it is essential as with Coates's scheme to work in reverse schedule order, unless otherwise instructed in the schedules.

As this scheme is still in the experimental stage and has not been fully published, it will suffice for now to draw attention to a number of new features additional to those already mentioned. The first is the attempt to make the scheme much more international by the appearance at 789, after the composer facet, of other traditions of music. It is argued quite correctly that the vast bulk of music and literature on music found in libraries belongs to the western art 'classical' tradition. The decision to give most of the 780 schedule to this tradition is therefore soundly based on literary warrant. All other traditions are placed in 789 following composers and can be subdivided by the same subdivisions as those used for classical music in 780—88. If a library specialises in one of these other music traditions it can use the 780—88 for that tradition and place classical music in 789 or elsewhere.

An examination of the literature suggested to the compilers that the traditions in 789 would best be divided by stylistic level which distinguishes folk, popular and art music. *Folk music* is defined as the musical tradition of a particular culture, which is free from contamination or acculturation with the music of other cultures. *Popular music* is defined as that which bears influences of other cultural groups than the one in which it appears, jazz being a particularly good example. *Art music* can be found particularly in Western Europe and parts of Asia, where society is settled and develops art forms which need refinement and appreciation, rather than immediate emotional response, in order to give pleasure. These three terms are in no sense used as value judgment on the music concerned, but are used to define origins in order to attempt a satisfactory distinction for the purposes of arranging material in libraries.

While this approach represents a major step forward in libraries' treatment of other forms of music than western classical, it is doubtful if the Phoenix schedules as they stand at present in 789 would cope with the complex problems of the various other music traditions. It seems inappropriate to use subdivisions devised for western classical music for totally different traditions. It may also seem confusing on the shelves to have all these traditions appearing in 789 alongside composers. This seems almost to relegate the whole of music to 789. Thirdly while it is probably true that material in most libraries is at the present time largely concerned with classical music, it is doubtful whether this is true of actual publications. It is to be hoped that library acquisitions will soon reflect the actual publishing proportions and the dominance accorded to western classical music in libraries will disappear. Finally the schedules given in the draft, which are presumably only outline, must surely be subjected to close critical examination not just by librarians but also by experts in each tradition. The jazz schedule at 789.6 indicates, for example, some acquaintance with the Langridge scheme for jazz discussed in chapter four. The Phoenix scheme uses *style* as the primary facet for jazz, which Langridge suggests for arranging recordings, but for the literature he suggests *musicians* as the primary facet. This is surely more soundly based on literary warrant. Perhaps the only solution for music of other traditions is to divorce them completely from classical music and provide separate schedules compiled with the help of experts.

Another feature of Phoenix 780 is the adoption of theHornbostel-Sachs classification for instruments discussed below (chapter five). This is the scheme generally used by ethnomusicologists in their work, and it is essential that such a system be used if the attempt to cater for other traditions is to have any meaning. The Hornbostel-Sachs scheme has been modified appropriately to cater for the particular needs of western classical music. For example 787 Stringed instruments adjusts the Hornbostel-Sachs arrangement to allow for a conventional European arrangement of the violin and viol families.

Finally an attempt has been made to systematise the arrangement of composers in a fuller way than was achieved by Coates in BCM. In the introduction three possible methods are set out, two using a pure number notation and one a mixed notation. The latter has been adopted for the scheme. For example:

789	DF	Debussy
	DH	Delius
	DR	Donizetti

Symbols from 780 – 788 are added as instructed in the introduction. Thus Donizetti: operas would be 789DR21 from 782.1 opera. The mixed notation may not be liked in practice by librarians to whom the pure notation of DC is one of its valuable features.

In conclusion, it must be stressed that Phoenix 780 is a draft scheme and that much work remains to be done, particularly in testing the practical use of the schedules in libraries and the compilation of bibliographies. This has already been done and revised schedules are now (November 1977) being examined by the DC Editorial Committee. It is a fine achievement.

The McColvin scheme

The task of reclassifying a library is a large one, but if librarians feel unable to undertake this work for the whole library they may find it possible at least for the music class, for which Lionel McColvin devised a special scheme using the decimal notation. This was originally printed in his book *Music libraries* published in 1937 (Grafton) and reprinted in the new edition revised by Jack Dove in 1965 (Deutsch). It is this scheme which influenced the formation of BCM and is in use in a modified form at the Central Music Library in London. It is a very simple scheme and has much to commend it to the librarian who is dissatisfied with DC but not prepared to use BCM.

Music is classed at 780–782, while the literature occupies the rest of the division (ie 783–789). Vocal music comes first at 780 and is subdivided into secular and sacred. Secular songs are arranged according to the number of voices.

780.3	Songs by individual composers A–Z
780.41	Duets – mixed voices – by composer A–Z
780.42	Duets – female voices – by composer A–Z
780.44	Trios, quartets etc also subdivided by type of voice and then by composer A–Z

Sacred music is arranged by form.

Instrumental music (solo and duet) is arranged in the order: wind, string (ie plucked), bowed, keyboard. Music for piano and another instrument goes under the other instrument, but music for two instruments, neither of which is the piano, is placed under the one with the higher average compass or the less common where they have comparable compass. This is a curious method. Surely it is easier to have an automatic rule such as placing under the one listed first in the schedules. Solos and duets are followed by chamber music and orchestral music. Miniature scores are arranged separately at 782.99 with no indication of the sub-arrangement in the outline schedules, although in volume two of *Music libraries* they are arranged alphabetically by composers. (Incidentally the running title 'music scores' in volume two of this work which continues to 789.98 must be a misprint and should be ignored.)

Opera appears at 780.7 quite conveniently separated from other secular vocal music to place it near instrumental music with which it is closely associated. If this was the reason for this arrangement, it is difficult to understand why the order of sacred and secular under vocal music was not reversed, to give the order:

780	Sacred music
780.5	Solo vocal music
780.7	Opera
781	Instrumental music

Arrangements are always classified under the instrument for which the piece is arranged, with no attempt to specify the original instrument. Nor is any attempt made to specify form under individual instruments. It is claimed by Jack Dove (page forty-eight of new edition) that it is nearly impossible to separate forms, but this is not really so in the case of clearly defined forms where the composer has deliberately written in a form such as sonata. To separate here would appear to be useful, especially where the material available is as numerous as is the music for piano.

With the addition of places for the foci in such facets as *elements, forms, space* and *time* the literature section follows the same order as that for the music. It is a simpler and much better arranged classification for the literature than that provided in DC. It is infortunate that the new editions of both schemes still fail to make any adequate provision for the literature of jazz. McColvin has dance band, dance music, jazz, swing and pops all at 786.9 with no attempt at subdivision. The inclusion of these very different forms under the one head is an indication of lack of understanding of this important division of music, in which research is as detailed and as busy as elsewhere. To the specialist it is as foolish to class jazz and pops together as it is to place opera and the mass in the same division.

However this is a practical scheme designed to offer a substitute for the confusion which abounds in class 780 of DC, and in this it succeeds admirably. In the examination of DC not too much emphasis was placed on the failings of the American scheme as these are self evident when the shelves of most of the public libraries in the United Kingdom are inspected. It is perhaps sufficient criticism that Lionel McColvin found it necessary to devise his own scheme and that the resulting improvement in the arrangement is immediately evident, whatever minor criticisms there may be of the McColvin scheme.

The Universal Decimal Classification

The English full edition of UDC 78 was first published in 1971 by the British Standards Institution. It is an interesting example of a scheme produced by a committee. The fact that the International Association of Music Libraries was not one of the organisations represented on the committee, while the Commonwealth Agricultural Bureau, the Department of Trade and Industry, and the Science Museum Library were, is noted without comment.

It is essential to use the full 780 schedules in conjunction with the *Abridged English edition*, BS 1000A, which gives the abridged schedules for the whole of knowledge. *The guide to the Universal Decimal Classification* (BS 1000C) is also a useful aid to correct classification by the scheme. It is also necessary to consult *Extensions and corrections to the UDC* which appears half yearly and contains full details of all authorised additions and corrections to the scheme. Major adjustments to the order have to be done by international agreement, but corrections to terminology and translation in the English edition can be made by the British Standards Institution.

It is well know that UDC is based on the Dewey Decimal Classification, but does not maintain the rule of three figure integrity of the original scheme. Hence 78 for Music, not 780. It is particularly useful for the classification of documents, and, while it is in some respects an enumerative scheme, it has such great flexibility that it is possible if so desired to express any concept contained within a document. When coupled with a carefully compiled subject index the scheme is capable of providing access to documents in depth. However, it is essential not to overdo this aspect and to work with a clear citation order for combining numbers, appropriate to the library or organisation concerned. The numbers produced by the scheme can be very long indeed, so much so that it is impossible to mark all the parts on a document. Thus 785.11.089.7:786.24 MOZART would be the symbol for a piano reduction (four hands) of Mozart's symphonies, made up of the following foci:

785.11	Symphonic music
.089.7	Piano reduction
786.24	For piano, four hands
Mozart	Mozart.

On the document it would be possible just to use 785.11 or 785.11.089.7. Then in the catalogue it would be necessary to indicate this by underlining that part of the notation used for filing.

785.11.089.7 : 786.24 Mozart

Like DC this scheme does not separate the literature about music from the scores. A book on the Mozart symphonies would be classed at 785.11 MOZART. This is unfortunate as it can lead to confusion and fails to recognise the physical nature of the material. Further it will be noted from the example above that the composer facet appears in both *scores* and *works on*, but, while it is secondary in *works on*, it is last in *scores*, It seems that under symphonies all the different kinds of score are collocated first. Thus using the subdivisions of the special auxiliary .089 the following can be expressed for example under any form:

.61	Conductors' scores
.62	Original scores
.63	Miniature scores
.64	Parts
.7	Piano reductions, including vocal scores.

This implies an order on the shelves where all symphonic music is arranged together, then subdivided by kind of score, whereas most music libraries would appear to arrange the same kinds of score together, irrespective of the musical form.

The outline of the class is as follows, with examples of foci in each class:

781	General theory of music
.41	Harmony
.61	Composition

.7	Theory and forms of national music of individual countries
782/785	Kinds of music
782	Dramatic music
783	Sacred music
784	Vocal music
785	Instrumental music
786/789	Music for individual instruments
786	Keyboard
787	Strings
788	Wind
789	Percussion

At one time a variety of devices were used for expressing relationships eg +1:, but in the 78 Music full schedules it is recommended that maximum use be made of the colon sign of relation. In fact it is perfectly possible to use this now as the only device for expression of relationship.

Duet for cello and flute

785.72	Duet
787.3	Cello
788.5	Flute

785.72:787.3:788.5.

This is to be preferred to 785.72:787.3+788.5.

There is a different relationship between 785.72 and 787.3 from that between 787.3 and 788.5, but the difference is of no significance for arrangement and it is simpler to have one device.

The common auxiliaries are used throughout the scheme to be applied to any basic numbers, unless the main table has provision for some other way of expressing the particular concept. They cover such approaches as language, form (ie general forms, not musical), place and time. Their use is fully explained in the guide and the abridged edition and they demonstrate again the very real flexibility this scheme possesses.

The special auxiliaries are applicable only to those sections of the scheme indicated. Examples of these in music are:

.067	Sociological aspects
.071.22	Concert tours
.082/.086	Forms of instrumental works
.087	Forms in relation to the instruments
.089	Format of published musical works

.087 covers such concepts as the number of instruments and the kind of voice.

65

The order of application of all these devices is main number — special auxiliaries — common auxiliaries (viewpoint — place — time — form — language). The basic filing order for documents proceeds from the general to the particular. Thus an item with only a main number precedes an item having a common auxiliary added which precedes a number having a direct decimal division:

781.61	Composition in general
781.61 : 782.1	Composition in relation to opera
781.61 (45)	Composition in Italy (common)
781.61.072.4	Composition adjudicators (special)
781.632	Orchestration (subdivision)

Biography is classed at 92:78, but in a special library this could be reversed 78:92 eg: 78:92 BEETHOVEN. Alternatively the common auxiliary (092) could be used: 78(092) BEETHOVEN

While there is no prescribed citation order for class 78 it is possible using *The guide*, the *Abridged edition*, and the examples given in the schedules of the class to work out a policy for application. A number of other schemes have seen the composer facet as having primacy in the *works on* section. In UDC this is not so. Entry of such works is made under the topic with the final principle of division being allocated to the composer facet:

Critical reviews of the opera Salome by Richard Strauss

782.1	Grand opera
.072.3	Criticism

STRAUSS, RICHARD, SALOME. Salome by Richard Strauss

782.1.072.3   Strauss, Richard, Salome.

Rehearsals of Strauss's Salome will go at

782.1.091.2   STRAUSS, RICHARD, SALOME.

Books on the opera in general will go at

782.1   STRAUSS, RICHARD, SALOME.

Following the earlier example of a piano reduction of Mozart's symphonies, a similar treatment of Salome would be placed at

782.1.089.7 : 786.24   STRAUSS, RICHARD, SALOME.

This would mean that all material relating to Salome would be scattered throughout the class. It also implies that an approach to the material via criticism of opera in general is more likely than by criticism of a particular opera.

Examples given under the special auxiliary .088 Transcriptions to any other medium without other alteration appear to conflict with the earlier Mozart example given in the introduction to the class. At .088

a very similar examples is given:

Arrangement of L van Beethoven's symphonies for piano (four hands).
This is given the class mark

785.11 BEETHOVEN 088.786.24.

To clarify the two chains are shown side by side.

785.11	Symphonies	785.11	
.089.7	Piano reductions	**BEETHOVEN**	
786.24	For piano four hands	.088	Transcriptions
MOZART		786.24	For piano four hands

In the Mozart chain the reduction or transcription is expressed by
using a focus from the facet *published format*, while in the Beethoven this
is achieved by using .088. The terminology at .088 seems to imply that no
alteration other than transcriptions has occurred in the Beethoven, and
hence presumably that alteration has taken place in the Mozart? But why
a different citation order for each example? Further under .088 the user
is referred to 78.083.82 Transcriptions, paraphrases, with no indication
as to the distinction between the two places. 78.083 is Other shorter
forms, and transcriptions here appears alongside Suites, variations, overtures, toccatas, medleys, which is an odd collection anyway. It is obvious
that any library using the scheme would have to decide on its own citation
order and definitions of terminology.

It will have been noticed that titles of works and composers' names are
used as a part of the notation. The use of names in this way is a fairly
common practice throughout UDC. As far as composers are concerned
there is no particular problem, but in using titles the fundamental problem in cataloguing music has to be met. This is quite simply that it is not
always very easy to decide what is the precise title of a work. Care will
have to be taken therefore to ensure that the title chosen for the notation
agrees with the title chosen for the uniform title in the catalogue entry.

Vocal music has the same unfortunate arrangement of the main divisions
as that used in DC, so that what are in effect the subdivisions 782 Dramatic music and 783 Sacred music appear before the main division 784
Vocal music. By use of the special auxiliary 78.087.6 and its subdivisions
similar specificity to that in BCM can be achieved:

Songs for contralto and tenor

784.3	Songs, ballads, lieder, arias, romances
.087.62	Duets
.612.6	Contralto
.613.1	Tenor
784.3.087.62.26.31	

Christmas carols for unaccompanied male voices

784.1	Unaccompanied vocal music
.087.683	Men's choirs
783.651.2	Christmas carols

784.1.087.683 : 783.651.2.

The general structure of the scheme would seem to suggest a preferred order might be

783.651.2 : 784.1.087.683

However, entry directly under the medium seems more satisfactory as a general principle. Incidentally the scheme makes the curious assumption that all carols are Christmas carols and that they are all sacred, as 783 is Sacred music. There is no way of expressing, say, Easter carols, but the general arrangement of sacred music is also unsatisfactory eg:

783.2	Liturgical music
.21	Masses. Communion services
.22	Common of the mass
.23	Liturgical music for special occasions
.24	Choral services
.25	Congregational singing
.26	Litanies
.27	Psalms
.28	Liturgical plays
.29	Masses for the dead, High masses

There would seem to be some difficulty here in deciding where the music of the mass should be placed, especially as provision is also made under 783 to divide by colon combination to class 2 to express music of individual rites eg Catholic church music 783:282.

Under instrumental music great specificity is possible. As the example for flute and cello given earlier (page 65) shows, the primary facet is size of ensemble, subdivided by kind of instrument. It is possible to express individual instruments in an ensemble if required:

Quartet for piano, violin, cello and flute

785.74	Quartet
786.2	Piano
787.1	Violin
787.3	Cello
788.5	Flute

785.74 : 786.2 : 787.1 : 787.3 : 788.5.

As can be seen the notation here is forward, not retroactive, as in most other modern schemes. If there are two of any instrument the number is given twice. Thus if the work had included two violins rather than violin and cello the notation would have been:

785.74 : 786.2 : 787.1 : 787.1 : 788.5.

The parts can be classed separately at the instrument's number:

Violin parts in quartets

787.1	Violin
.03	Special auxiliary = 'by'
.087.34	Quartets
787.1.03.087.34	

It is difficult to imagine any library wanting to separate parts of a work in this way.

For an international scheme UDC 78 is astonishingly dominated by western European classical music, although under 781.7 Theory and form of national music of individual countries can be expressed.

Folk music of Iran

781.7	Theory and forms of national music
(55)	Iran (common auxiliary of place)
784.4	Folk songs
781.7 (55) : 784.4	

There appears to be no way of expressing folk music, only folk song.

Jazz receives scant treatment, appearing at 785.161 Music for dance bands, jazz bands, and under 785.1 Instrumental music for orchestra, while popular music receives no mention at all. Apparently jazz is seen as an instrumental form. Blues appear at 78.085.323 under Dance forms, which is a quite astonishing allocation when it is seen to be in array with polkas, mazurkas, tangos and foxtrots.

The scheme is an interesting one and has several useful features like the use of .089 to express format of published musical work, but in practice it seems to show little awareness of the nature of published music, nor of the way the material is actually handled in libraries. A library adopting the scheme would need to edit it carefully, produce its own citation orders and give very clear instructions to classifiers.

The Bliss Bibliographic Classification (Original edition)

It is hard to reconcile the lifetime spent by Henry Evelyn Bliss on the study of classification and the compilation of his own scheme with the very small number of libraries now using the scheme. It seems unlikely that many libraries will adopt it in the future, and yet so important is the study of classification made by Bliss that some account of his work on music must be given.

One of the most interesting features of BC is the lengthy discussion of the problems of classifying music. This can be found in the introduction to his volume three, chapter five, section three and in the introductory material to class VV. Briefly, it may be said that Bliss is concerned with what the term 'music' means basically and to different people. He shows that music has many meanings such as 'sound', 'composition', 'rendition'. He is aware of the cross-classification which is implicit in such concepts as 'singing a song' as opposed to 'the song that is sung'.

To turn to the schedules, MUSIC is in class V — AESTHETIC ARTS at VV. A synopsis can be found at the beginning of VV which gives a very clear picture of how the subject is organised.

As with LC and BCM, music scores and music literature are clearly separated:

VV — VW Music literature

VX Scores and Records

In a note under VX Bliss does suggest that the two can be combined at VV, but he obviously does not favour this. Records can go at VX5 and, if wished can be classified in the same way as the scores. It is unlikely that any gramophone librarian would want to do this.

As in other parts of BC, alternative treatment is allowed in some divisions. For example, biography (VV9) may be arranged alphabetically by composer subdivided by a systematic schedule (no 7) provided at L9 BIOGRAPHY. This is not so detailed as the table for Wagner in LC but is more practical and can be applied easily to any composer. It might well be used for division of biographical material even if the BC scheme as a whole is not adopted. Alternatively biography can be arranged by country, subdivided alphabetically, or the arrangement can be chronological. In either case general systematic schedules for the space and time facets are provided.

The facets techniques, elements and forms all come together in a somewhat confused way under the general head:

VWD   Arts of composing and producing music.

So that under

VWF   Composition (*technique*)

come such *elements* as

VWFB   Notation

VWFC   Staff

while under

VWI   Counterpoint (*element*)

come

| VWIL | Fugue (*form*) |
| VWIP | Polyphonic music (to judge by definitions in dictionaries of music this is an imprecise term, but counterpoint is generally seen as a subdivision of polyphony). |

It must be apparent from the examples that the notation as in BCM and LC, is not expressive. The relationship of subjects as shown in these examples is based on the layout of the schedules.

Having dealt with the art of composition, Bliss next brings in STUDY and TEACHING, following by PUBLICATION AND RECORDING OF MUSIC, then VOCAL AND INSTRUMENTAL MUSIC. His arrangement here is curious. Under:

| VWU | Wind instruments |

come

VWUN	Percussion instruments
VWUU	Chamber music
VWUV	String quartets

The philosophical approach is seen in his arrangement of vocal music before instrumental music. He also makes provision for completely separate classes:

| VWW | Religious music |
| VWY | Popular music |

Is it possible to have religious instrumental music? No, as Bliss recognises by not separating the music into religious and secular scores; but he does provide this place for literature discussing the subject. JAZZ comes under ORCHESTRAL MUSIC and not under POPULAR MUSIC.

The scores at VX are arranged:

VXH	Vocal scores
VXI	Duets
VXJ	Concert and chamber
VXK	Religious
VXL	Dramatic and operatic
VXM	Orchestral music
VXN	Chamber music
VXO – VXY	Individual instruments

Schedule 22 under PIANO can be used to subdivide any instrument:

VXP	Piano
VXPI	Piano sonatas (schedule 22)
VXT	Flute

Apply schedule 22:

| VXTI | Flute sonata |

71

This schedule provides a very simple way of dealing with compound subjects. Incidentally, the form CONCERTO will be found under both VXM and schedule 22. It is not indicated in the schedules, but presumably full scores are put under ORCHESTRA and arrangements for solo instrument and piano go under the instrument.

It would not be reasonable with this scheme, any more than with LC, to apply facet techniques to criticism of the arrangement of music literature, but once again a facet formula would be useful in using the scheme. However, commenting on the arrangement of scores, Dr Ranganathan's theories can be used, as Bliss has clearly applied these. The main tables are arranged by instrument and are subdivided by schedule 22 to give form. Thus in dealing with compound subjects the facet formula is clearly: instruments, form.

The facet size is covered by VXN, although here instruments other than strings receive rather poor treatment.

This scheme reveals very careful thought behind its construction. Unfortunately the layout of the schedules gives evidence of haste. There is no symbol for guitar scores, for example, although provision is made for the instrument under the literature. It seems likely that this scheme, unlike that other excellent classification, the subject classification of James Duff Brown, will receive both regular and systematic revision. This is good, for it has much to comment it, and with revision its simple arrangement of scores would be most effective. Its notation, by using letters in preference to figures, can express compound subjects briefly.

The Bliss Classification revision

This is the work of my colleague, Jack Mills, and when completed will be the most modern general classification in existence. It takes full account of modern classification theory and attempts to preserve the best features of Bliss's work. The work is being published in parts and to date the schedules for music have not appeared, although they exist in penultimate draft form. It is on the basis of this draft that the following comments are made, as it is not anticipated that there will be any major revision as a result of comments received from those to whom it has been circulated.

Like Phoenix 780 for Dewey the new Bliss music schedules are very firmly based on the work of Eric Coates for BCM. Thus it is now a fully faceted scheme with citation order for works about music and works of music which are almost identical to those in BCM:

The citation order for works about music is Composer – Instrument (including voice) – Musical form (eg sonata, fugue) – Musical element (eg tonality) – Musical character (eg military music, dance music) –

Musical technique (eg performing) — Musical theory (this appears to be the equivalent of BCM's phase relationships—see below).

Works of music has the same citation order as above but omits the composer facet, therefore Instrument is the primary facet. It is unlikely of course that Technique and Theory will be used very much for scores, except for a limited number of instructional pieces.

The schedule order is the reverse of the citation order in VX (scores) but in VV/VW the original use of VV9 for Composers was maintained to help those libraries already using Bliss. This results in the special not always following the general: eg a study of Beethoven's symphonies in VV9 BJ, MM, while a study of symphonies in general is VVM M. In nearly all other cases the notation is, as one would expect, retroactive. Combination is achieved simply by taking the letter(s) following the VW or VX in the notation for the foci earlier in the schedule and adding them to the notation for the primary term:

VWB G   Performance
VWF O   Opera
VWF OBG   Opera performance

This can be done automatically except where instructions to the contrary appear in the schedules.

Perhaps the most interesting feature of the new schedules is the attempt made to deal with non-European music. In the tradition of Bliss's original concept alternative methods of treatment are provided.

Most of the literature in BC libraries concerns music in the European tradition and a work on, say, musical form will be treated as a general work on that subject although it implicitly assumes the European tradition. Libraries wishing to make the distinction between 'general' in the true sense and 'general' in relation to the European tradition may use VV (ie VV 1/9, A/Z) for the former and VW only for European material strictly. In such cases the detail enumerated in VW may be added—eg VVC R Religious music in general (dealing with European and non-European material). [VWC R Religious music in the European tradition].

The theoretically accurate schedule called for in a truly international classification of music would be, in outline:

VV 1/9   Music in general — common subdivisions
VV A/Z   Music in general — theory, techniques, character, etc.
VWA/X   European tradition
VWY   Afro-American tradition
VWZ   Non-European tradition [other traditions?]

Whether scores are collocated with the system ('tradition') or kept together is essentially a matter of library policy here.

Alternatively, many libraries will prefer to continue to use the division of VW both for truly general works and for 'general' works which in fact assume or imply the European traidion. A major reason for this would be to avoid separating works on topics (eg dance music) in the European tradition from works on the same topic dealing mainly but not entirely with the European tradition in it.

It is likely, however, that libraries using the alternative—ie using VW for all materials except specifically non-European ones (which would go at VWZ) will prefer to retain the common subdivisions and the composer facet of Music literature at VV 1/9, A/Z. (From the introduction to schedules)

A further alternative scheme for the treatment of non-European traditions is provided by a choice between VWZ as above and the use of existing Bliss provision of the whole of VVA/VVZ for local division. Non-European material could be classed there. In this case number building would not be retroactive but forward:

VVq — India
VWE — Musical form
VVq E — Form in Indian music

Once again general would follow special. There would also be some deliberate inconsistency here as in the European tradition place would be the secondary facet.

VWE OAK   Form in German music

Afro-American music has, as an essential feature, a very large element of improvisation, which makes the music score relatively unimportant. Therefore the sharp distinction between scores and works about music is not made at VWY, which is based on Derek Langridge's classification for jazz (see chapter four). In this all Afro-American forms and derivatives are covered but jazz is treated as the preferred category and assigned the main notation VW 1/9, A/V. Then Jazz composition would be VWY BB not VWY XBB. The arrangement is parallel with that under VW as far as possible. Thus VWE is Forms, while VWY E is Forms under Afro-American music, with the addition of VWY EN Special jazz forms eg Call and response, Riffs, Blues as a form, Rags as a form. The essential features from the Langridge scheme are the treatment of musicians as the primary facet (VWY V) and the adoption of the styles facet (VWY U). Additional is the provision of places for Caribbean (VWY YC) and Latin America and South America (VWY YE). Both schemes cater for Popular

74

musicians (in Bliss VWY YV). Once again this is the primary facet under Popular music and can presumably be subdivided by the whole scheme, as can Caribbean, Latin America, and South America, although no specific instructions are given to this effect. Like that of the Phoenix 780 (DC) schedules this is a serious attempt to deal with traditions other than the classical western European one, but while the revised Bliss is a better attempt at coping with the problem than that of Phoenix 780 the same general comment made on page 60 applies equally to the Bliss revision.

This country has become especially rich with other cultures since the last war and it is a pity that librarians have generally failed, until recently, to recognise their existence. But attitudes are changing, greater provision of non-western cultural material is being made in some areas and classification schemes will surely have to take account of this. Thus the revised Bliss music schedules should have developed schemes for other traditions fashioned by consultation with experts as occurred in the case of jazz.

The outline of the revised Bliss schedules will give some indication of its structure and its similarity to BCM and Phoenix 780 (DC). An asterisk against a term indicates that the basic symbol is the same as in the first edition.

VV 1/6	Common subdivision*
7	Phase relationships
8	History*
9	Biography of composers* (Using BCM codes — an unfortunate decision as these are one of the weak parts of BCM)
VVA/Z	History by locality*
	Alternative placing for non-European music
VWA	Theory of music
	Divide like whole classification
	VWA B Physics
VWB	Composing and producing (techniques)
	(When elements from this facet are combined together, it is to be done forward, not retroactively).
VWC	Musical character (BCM sense)
VWD	Elements
VWE	Forms
VWF/VWX	Music for particular media (works on)
VWF/K	Vocal music
VWL/X	Instrumental music
VWX	Folk music in the European tradition.

	Divide like 'Art' music so far as is necessary—eg Record-
	ing folk music VWX BR.
VWX	Afro-American music
VWZ	Non-European music
VX	Music : scores and parts
VX2	Bibliography of scores.
VXA	Educational material
VXA X/Z	Collections
VXF/X	Music for particular media

Hopefully the examples worked throughout the explanation of the scheme will have demonstrated how it works. In fact the principle of combination is so similar to the one used in BCM that, having understood the one, there is little difficulty in understanding the other:

String quartet

BCM	BC		
RX	VXQ	Z	Bowed string instruments
NS	VXN	S	Quartets
RXNS	VXQ	ZNS	

Christmas carols for unaccompanied male voices

C/LF	VWC	S				Christmas
DP	VWG	S				Carols
EZ	VXG	Z				Unaccompanied choral works
G	VXH	S				Male voices
GEZ DP/LF	VXH	SGZ	GSC	S		

The notation for Bliss seems rather unwieldy in comparison with the equivalent one for BCM, but of course the latter is a specialist scheme and has the advantage of not having to express the concept Music.

The Bliss scheme is an interesting example of an attempt to turn a largely enumerative scheme into a faceted one. It is to be hoped that the printed schedules will contain more information on the correct method of combination under the instrument facet, when the two instruments in a duet belong either to the same family or to different families; unless the intention is to apply the retroactive principle strictly in all cases. If this is so then this departure from BCM practice should be clarified (see page 31). Further examples of how the scheme works for music would form a useful feature in the introduction to the music schedules. It will be a great loss if the revised scheme is not more widely used in libraries than the existing one, as it represents the consecutive collaboration of perhaps the finest minds on classification theory and practice of two generations.

Brown Subject Classification

James Duff Brown was an outstanding librarian in the period around the turn of the century. He had a considerable interest in music and was one of the earliest writers on music librarianship as well as compiling two very valuable reference books on music. He anticipated many ideas which were not developed by other librarians until much later. For example he saw immediately that the fundamental fault of the 1908 Anglo-American Cataloguing Code lay in its failure to deal with broad principles and its attempt to quote rules for every single case or situation that a cataloguer was likely to meet, thereby anticipating Seymour Libetzky's ideas by half a century. In his *Subject classification* he developed a scheme which operates very much like a faceted classification.

He disliked the approach of other classificationists such as Dewey, which provided for broad classes in which books had to be grouped by subject and purpose eg 600 Useful arts, technology. He maintained that an item could only be placed in one position on the shelves and therefore the classification ought to provide only one place for each subject. Thus in the subject classification Electricity is classed at C001 only; in DC it can be classed at either 537 or 621.3 according to the purpose of the book: either pure or applied science. Some texts cannot easily be so classified— they may, indeed, fulfil both criteria.

Brown also tried to place each activity with the science from which it stemmed. This produced some rather amusing (but, nevertheless, sensible) results:

C 200	Heat
C 225	Fire producers
C 230	Fire extinction
C 231	Fire engines

in DC fire engines would be classified at 628.92, with Engineering.

The arrangement devised by Brown means that the class Fine arts, widely used in other schemes, is completely scattered in his. Thus Drawing and Painting come at A 600 after Geometry at A 500, Architecture at B 300 after Civil engineering at B 200 and Music at C 400 after Acoustics at C 300.

The scheme is divided into four broad areas

1	Matter	(eg B – C – D	Physical sciences)
2	Life	(eg E – F	Biological sciences)
3	Mind	(eg J – K	Philosophy and Religion)
4	Record	(eg M – N	Language and Literature)

Music is therefore not very logically placed within this very broad framework, however appropriate it may be for it to follow acoustics.

Like Dewey, Brown made no separation of music scores from music literature, not even providing a method as DC does for making a distinction in the notation. There are a number of interesting features in the class and it is a pity that the scheme as a whole has been neglected through the failure to provide some system for keeping it up to date. As the only British library classification of all knowledge it merits a better fate.

Theoretical subjects come first in the schedules and there is little to comment on here but at C 440 Musical forms there appear lists of instrumental and dance forms, which can be combined with the instrumental foci coming later in the schedules to provide compound numbers. The notation is clumsy, but the principle formed the basis of subsequent developments in BCM. For example:

Sonata for piano

    piano   C647

    sonata   C442

    C647 + 442

Studies for flute

    Flute   C687

    studies   C459

    C687 + 459

It will be noticed that the combination is in reverse schedule order and that the initial C is dropped from the form. Brown makes it clear in the introduction that compound numbers are to be formed in this way for music scores. For literature on the sonata C 442 is to be used. He does not make clear where literature on the piano sonata is to be placed, but any library using the scheme could develop its own rule.

Duets for instruments are to be entered under the solo instrument:

Duet for oboe and piano

    C 703   Oboe

    C 647   piano

    C 703 + 647

Unfortunately no guidance is given on entering music for two equal instruments eg flute and oboe. Again local rules would have to be framed.

The arrangement of the instrument class is by method of sound production, which gives:

    C 603   String instruments (bowed)

    C 620   String instruments (plectral)

    C 640   String instruments (keyboard)

    C 655   Wind instruments (cup-blown)

    C 690   Wind instruments (reed blown)

    C 715   Wind instruments (keyed)

This means that piano is classed under String instruments (keyboard) at C647, flute under Wind instruments (cup blown) at C 687 and organ under Wind instruments (keyed) at C 725. Once again this is scientifically logical, but somewhat curious for a scheme designed essentially for classical music.

Chamber music at C770 is divided by size of performing group, with no attempt at indication of the instruments making up the groups.

C 771	Nonets
C 772	Octets
C 777	Trios

The arrangement of vocal music is unsatisfactory and does not seem to be as carefully thought out as that for instrumental music. Thus some vocal forms associated with operas and cantatas appear at C500 eg C 501 Arias, while other forms such as oratorios, cantatas and odes are at C535 — C550. Then dramatic music including opera, ballet and film music appears right at the end of the class immediately after instruments, orchestral and chamber music. If the logic was that such vocal forms also involve large scale use of instruments, this is surely equally true of oratorios and masses. Further in the middle of the vocal section appear:

C 505	Analysis of forms and compositions
C 531	Conducting

Brown cannot have meant that these should only apply to vocal forms, but that is the implication.

Individual voices are classed at C520:

C 521	Soprano
C 525	Tenor

No indication on combination is given.

Some compound subjects can be expressed by use of the categorical tables, which provide a complete list of qualifying factors which can be combined with any number in the main tables. Among the more usual items such as

.1	Bibliography
.41	Biography
.67	Lectures

appear the following music topics

.257	Acoustics
.258	Tone
.259	Pitch
.260	Music
.261	Scales
.267	Songs
.269	Operas

79

.270 Oratorios etc

These can therefore be added to numbers for instruments, voices etc.

Songs for soprano

Soprano	C521
Songs	.267

C521.267

Presumably it is also possible to express opera arias by using .269 from the categorical tables, but not cantata arias as no number for cantatas is provided in them.

Brown includes also systems for expressing place and time, as well as biographical tables, but the use of all these is voluntary. Brown himself seems to have favoured simple alphabetical order whenever possible, an approach which would surely commend itself to many music librarians.

There is much to criticise in the scheme, but it has been used successfully in a number of British public libraries. It is included here to illustrate how important it was to the development of faceted schemes, in that the germ of the idea is clearly there. The scheme could be revised and much fuller use made of the categorical tables to effect combinations of elements in compound subjects. It is a very simple scheme to use. Perhaps with some classificationists feeling that depth classification has gone too far it may come back in to use again in a revised form.

Colon Classification

One reviewer of the first edition of this book expressed disappointment that the Colon Classification devised by Dr Ranganathan had not been examined. The reason should be obvious even on a cursory glance at the tables, as class NR Music has not been completed. The outline and citation order is given, but the foci under the music and instrument facets are incomplete and the technique facet is to be worked out. It is difficult to comment on a scheme, the final form of which can only be surmised.

The main interest centres on the citation order which is provided and is

[P] , [P2]	Style
[P3]	Music
; [M]	Instrument
: [E] [2P]	Technique

Style is obtained by combining symbols from space and time facets. Thus Italian Baroque music would be NR 52,K

NR	Music
52	Italy from space facet
K	1600–1699 from time facet

The space facet is not fully developed for all areas in the world. Thus there is no symbol for any town in Italy, France or many other countries. Nevertheless the device for expressing style is a very simple and effective one, and if the relevant facets are completed the approach could be very useful for libraries concerned with enthnomusicology.

Music [P3] is an odd collection if isolates:

1	Word, libretto
18	Notation
2	Form
6	Keeping time, *talam*
91	Dramatic music
92	Orchestral music

It is difficult to see how they are meant to form a homogeneous group until the facet is fully developed, but to add dramatic music to the Italian Baroque example is very simple:

NR52, k 91

Instrument [M] is very incomplete. Under 2 Wind instrument, for example, come

21	Pipe
22	Flute
23	Organ
24	Claironet (sic)
25	Oboe
26	Bassoon
27	Bagpipe
28	Trumpet
29	Others
291	Harmonium

This implies a principle of division by method of producing the sound rather than by method of playing, which is more usual in other general schemes. The piano appears at 34 under Stringed instruments. The trumpet in dramatic music of the Italian Baroque would be

NR52, K91; 28

Vocal music has not been developed at all, although notation at 91 is provided in the Instrument facet. The curious printing of the scheme makes it appear to be a subdivision of Percussion instruments.

It is not even clear from the tables whether the class NR is intended for music scores or literature or both. The citation order implies a research approach rather than a performance approach. It is an interesting scheme in its implications. It is to be earnestly hoped that it will be developed, as the Colon Classification is a very effective scheme in general and very simple to apply once the basic rules have been learned. What is there so far could be a firm base from which to compile a scheme to cover all forms of music from all countries.

CHAPTER FOUR

A SPECIAL SCHEME FOR JAZZ

IN GENERAL the treatment of jazz and other forms of so called 'popular' music by libraries is highly unsatisfactory. Most music librarians are trained in the western classical tradition and, while they may have an interest in popular forms, this is frequently not intense enough to meet the demands of the specialist in a particular form such as jazz or reggae. The failure of libraries in this respect is sometimes commented on ruefully or angrily in the correspondence columns of specialist journals. Such comment usually seems to suggest that where libraries are providing jazz recordings, for example, all too often the music included bears little resemblance to what a specialist would count as jazz. Sometimes there may be jazz enthusiasts working in other departments of the library, whose expertise is not used.

Not only does the selection of material related to all the popular forms need careful attention, but also each may require distinctive treatment in terms of cataloguing and arranging, if full use of it is to be made once it is added to the library. In describing each of the classification schemes reference has been made to the generally unsatisfactory treatment of jazz, as an example of a popular form which has produced a great deal of literature and is particularly associated with this century and the development of recorded sound. Jazz is the most accepted of all the popular forms, apart perhaps from folk, and if it is treated badly by classification schemes as indeed is folk music, what hope is there for the newer forms such as rock, progressive pop, reggae etc?

However, my colleague Derek Langridge, who combines the dual qualities of an enthusiasm for both jazz and classification, has produced very satisfactory detailed classifications for both jazz literature and jazz records. These can be found in his book *Your jazz collection* (London, Bingley; Hamden, Conn, Archon, 1970). As the title implies the book is intended primarily for the jazz collector but the classification schemes could be very satisfactorily adopted by libraries for their collections. The following brief comment will hopefully illustrate the usefulness of the two schemes.

83

Both are of course faceted schemes with retroactive notations. Letters are used for the notation, which is remarkably brief even when expressing fairly complex subjects.

Jazz literature

The citation order is musicians — styles — instruments and bands — the music (description, theory, analysis, criticism) — history — jazz life and environment — promotion, presentation and dissemination — persons and institutions — place — periods — reference books — forms.

The schedule order is therefore (with examples)

A	*Physical forms of materials*
Ab	Scores
Ac	Gramophone records
	Imaginative forms
Ar	Humour
Av	Short stories
B	*Reference works, composite works and introductions*
Bc	Dictionaries
By	Primers (including books for children)
Bz	Comprehensive surveys
C	*Periods*
Cf	Twenties
Ch	Modern period (for modern style see Rp)
Cm	Seventies
D – F	*Places*
G	*Persons and institutions*
	Used as subdivisions of the appropriate activities eg JnGv
	Recording companies
Gf	Young
Gv	Institutions etc.
H – J	*Promotion, presentation and dissemination of jazz*
Hr	Libraries
Jn	Recording companies
K	*Jazz life and environment*
Kg	Attitudes to jazz
Kk	Neglect
Ky	Kinds of audience
L	*History*
	For periods of jazz history divide by C.
	Relationships with other subjects
Lv	Comparison
Lw	Jazz influenced by –
M – N	*The music*
Mc	Creation

Mj	Uses of jazz
Nd	Performing
P	*Instruments and bands*
Pb	Bands (Individual bands S)
Pj	Woodwind section
R	*Styles*
Rc	Negro
Rj	Dixieland
S	*Musicians*
	Individuals arranged A – Z. Use first three letters of surname eg Snoo=Jimmy Noone
T	*Afro-American music*
	Subdivide by any preceding section (s)
Tg	Blues
V	*Popular music*
	For twentieth century popular forms influenced by Afro-American forms eg Skiffle VTgPy, where Tg=Blues and Py=Unorthodox, improvised instruments.
W	*European and other musical traditions*
	Use of the BCM schedules are recommended here.
X	*The arts*
Xm	*The humanities*
Y	*Social sciences*

The above outline together with the citation order should give some idea of the excellence of this scheme.

Langridge gives a long series of examples using the scheme in his book, so there seems little point in quoting further examples here. They demonstrate very clearly how the schedules work. Selecting Musicians as the primary facet for the literature is a parallel choice to Composers in BCM and BC for western classical music. In most cases it can be argued that through his improvisation technique the jazz musician is indeed the composer and therefore the comparison can be very precisely drawn.

Perhaps further comment should be made on the phase relationships. Comparison (Lv) can either be used to compare within jazz or outside. Thus a comparison of Louis Armstring and Henry Allen would be Sall Lv Sarm, while jazz compared to poetry will be LvXb (Xb being drawn from X The arts). These processes can be used with any of the symbols under phase relationships.

For recordings two alternative schemes are provided. The first arranges by style:

A	Collections
B	Traditional
J	Mainstream
M	Modern
R	Avant garde
T	Hybrids
V	Jazz of countries other than USA, subdivide alphabetically by country and then by style.
W	Afro-American folk music
X	Blues
Y	Ragtime
Z	Popular music

The second arranged by period:

A	Collections
AW	Early jazz
G	Swing period
K	Modern period
	etc as for styles arrangements.

The difficulty with the period arrangement is that styles are not confined to periods, therefore in the modern period one has to allow for the many different styles which flourished, so subdivisions under K are:

L	New Orleans
N	Dixieland
P	Mainstream
R	Modern

The styles arrangement certainly gives greater flexibility and it is interesting that, as has been noted, Phoenix 780 uses this facet as the primary facet for jazz literature. Literary warrant and the experience of libraries suggests that Langridge's choice for Musicians is more soundly based. His schemes for recordings are both simple and could be used in libraries having browser boxes or shelves for display and/or storage.

CHAPTER FIVE

THE CLASSIFICATION OF MUSICAL INSTRUMENTS

INSTRUMENTS are a major aspect of the performance and study of music. It is likely, as has already been stated, that in a library of performance material the primary approach will in most cases be by medium of performance. In the study of music the names of instruments are likely to be frequently sought terms and whatever other category of terms is used as primary search, it is highly probable that instruments will appear very early in the search pattern.

It follows therefore that the way in which music for instruments and books about them are arranged in libraries is very important. So far the schemes for music, whether special or general, have been very heavily biased towards western classical music. Indeed, most of them follow what is often loosely referred to as full score order: woodwind, brass, percussion, string. Within each group some general attempt to arrange according to pitch can be observed: violin, viola, cello, bass.

This works excellently as long as a library's collection is principally concerned with music for the normal instruments of the symphony orchestra. Trouble starts as soon as music for other instruments is added to stock. The saxophone has been in use now for over one hundred years, but the schemes are still undecided as to whether it is a member of the woodwind or brass family. It is played by vibrating a reed, but it is made of brass. So the schemes differ:

UDC		DC	
788.11/4	Brass instruments	788.5–788.9	Woodwind
788.43	Saxophone	788.66	Saxophone

LC and BC (original) agree with UDC, while BCM, DC Phoenix and BC (revised) agree with DC. Most saxophone players play clarinet and would therefore expect to find the music for both related.

The problem lies in the failure of some schemes to determine a consistent principle of division in this class. Is division by method of performance or by material of manufacture?

87

The widening of the scope of the service provided by music libraries to include popular forms and the music of other cultures means that much more serious attention to the classification of instrumental material will have to be given in the future. Enthnomusicologists have had to devote much time to the consideration of an appropriate scheme. When the comparative study of different musical cultures is at stake, it is necessary to devise a scheme that will take account of the extraordinary range of devices which man has manufactured in order to produce a musical sound. The schemes in all the western library classifications can only be described as primitive when they are set against the needs of the ethnomusicologist.

All credit is therefore due to the compilers of the Phoenix Dewey schedules for being the first to turn to the ethnomusicologist for guidance in devising schedules for the medium of performance division in their revision. The scheme which they used is that of Erich M von Hornbostel and Curt Sachs. This was originally published in *Zeitschrift für Ethnologie* 1914 vol 4 no 5 as *Systematik der Musikinstrumente Ein Versuch* and has been translated into English by Anthony Baines and Klaus P Wachsmann as *Classification of musical instruments* in the *Galpin Society journal* vol 14, pages 3–29. In outline it is easily available in *Musical instruments* (London, Horniman Museum and Library, 1970. 2nd edition). Definitions are very important in ethnomusicology and these were agreed for instruments in 1969 by the musical instrument committee of the International Council for Museums. Simplified versions for the general reader are given in the very useful Horniman guide.

The principle of division used in the Hornbostel–Sachs classification is acoustical. This produces four main classes:

Idiophones Instruments made of inherently resonant material, which are made to sound by percussion.

Membranophones Instruments in which the sound is produced by movement of a stretched membrane.

Aerophones Instruments in, through or around which a quantity of air is made to vibrate.

Cordophones Instruments which have one or more string, held at tension, which are sounded by plucking with the fingers or a plectrum, bowing, striking, friction, or occasionally by wind.

It is only possible here to give a broad outline of the grouping which results from this division. For a full scholarly translation of the tables readers are referred to the *Galpin Society journal* as indicated, and for a general explanation to the excellent Horniman guide. Equally useful and marvellously illustrated is *Musical instruments of the world* by the

Diagram Group (London, Paddington Press, 1976), which uses the Horn-bostel—Sachs classification for its arrangement and demonstrates clearly the relationship between the instruments of the western classical repertoire and others.

The scheme produces the following groupings:

1 Idiophones
 Struck
  Castanets
  Xylophones
  Bells
 Shaken
  Rattles
  Jingles
 Scraped
  Bore scrapers
  Washboards
 Plucked (also called Linguaphones)
  Jews's harps
  Musical box
 Friction
  Glass harmonica
  Musical saw
 Blown
  Blown sticks
  Blown plaques
2 Membranophones
 Struck drums
  Kettle drums
   Nakers
   Timpani
  Tubular drums
   Bass drum
  Frame drum
   Tambourine
 Friction drums
  Rommelpot (Europe)
  Whirled friction drum (England)
 Mirlitons
  Kazoo

3 Chordophones
    Simple Chordophone or zither (consists solely of a string bearer. Can have a resonator, which is not integral)
        Bow zither
            Musical bow
        Tube zither
        Raft zither (string bearer of canes tied like a raft)
        Board zither
         (Plucked)
            Psaltery
            Virginal
            Harpsichord
         (Struck)
            Dulcimer
            Clavichord
            Pianoforte
        Trough zither
        Frame zither
    Composite chordophones (string bearer and resonator organically united)
        Lute
         (Plucked)
            Lute
            Guitar
         (Bowed)
            Viol
            Violin
        Harps
        Harp lutes
4 Aerophones
    Free aerophones (vibrating air not confined by instrument)
        Free reed
            Reed organ
            Mouth organ
            Accordion
        Whirler aerophone
            Bull roarer
    Wind instruments proper (vibrating air confined in instrument)

Flute family (edge blown)
 Flute
 Recorder
Reedpipes
 Oboe
 Clarinet
 Saxophone
Trumpet family (cup blown)
 Trumpet
 Trombone
 Horn
Hybrid (vibrating air free and confined)
 Organ
 Bagpipe

As can be seen, the result of this classification by acoustical properties
is that the saxophone is quite clearly in the same family as the clarinet.
The separation of organ and piano is less satisfactory from the point of
view of libraries primarily concerned with western classical music. Phoenix
Dewey very sensibly recognises this and places them together:

786.2	Piano
.3	Clavichord
.4	Harpsichord
.5	Organ
.55	Reed organ
.57	Accordion

In no sense would it be practical to suggest that libraries should separate
organ music from piano music in order to conform with a theoretical
classification of musical instruments. Nevertheless, as has already been
said, the range of interest and demand is widening. The conference of the
International Association of Music Libraries in Mainz in 1977 gave further
evidence in some of the discussions of a growing interest in other forms
of music. Librarians may well have to adjust the bias of their collections in
the next few years and classification must keep pace. The work done by
ethnomusicologists may prove to be of great value in helping librarians
to adjust their collections to this shift in emphasis.

CHAPTER SIX

THE ARRANGEMENT OF SOUND RECORDINGS

MANY LIBRARIES now allow users to have direct access to records and cassettes in the same way as they have to books. Others still feel that it is wiser to hold those items for handling by staff only. In this event some kind of indicator system must be provided to enable enquirers to establish what is immediately available for loan. Some libraries display the record sleeves and the empty cassette containers. Others use some sort of catalogue; for example, cards for the recordings available can be shown on a display board.

The profession has rather abused the English language by referring to the situation when the recordings are not displayed openly as 'closed access', where the sleeves are displayed as 'partial access' and when the recordings are displayed as 'open access'.

In the case of closed access the simplest method of arrangement for the recordings is by the companies' catalogue numbers. These numbers are used throughout the trade, in all record reviews and in discographies; it follows that the users who borrow records will be familiar with them as a means of reference, as they are more than likely to buy recordings as well. They will know the difference in quality represented by SXL, ASD and SLPM, all of which are parts of catalogue numbers used by major companies, and it will not seem strange to them when they have to ask for a record by a number prefixed by such letters. In these circumstances there seems little point in a library adding its own accession number to be used as an arranging device.

Records in the BBC Gramophone Library are arranged first by the label eg Angel, Heliodor, and then by the catalogue number. This is a very simple system, but an equally simple method is to arrange directly by the catalogue number. Whichever of these systems is used, it will be more effective than one which is home-made. It has the added advantage for the users that the library's own catalogue can quite often be ignored. Users can come direct from a search in a trade catalogue, discography or record review to the librarian. Whereas, if an accession number is used, they must first find this by consulting the library's catalogue. In any event the indicator must also be consulted to establish what is 'in' the library.

The arrangement of the indicator cards is usually by composer or collection title, as appropriate, in the case of classical recordings, and by the name(s) of the performers(s) or groups or collection title, again as appropriate, in the case of popular forms. The arrangement has to be simple in this situation, as the cards on display are constantly changing as recordings are returned or borrowed.

In the case of partial or open access, the recordings or their containers are usually displayed in the same way as they are in shops ie in browser boxes for records and in racks for cassettes; although for the latter ordinary shelving is quite practical. To adopt the commercial method is an excellent idea and it is unlikely to result in any serious damage to the recordings. For classical music the arrangement in the browser boxes need be only into broad groups such as 'symphonies', 'concertos', 'chamber music' and 'lieder'. In most libraries the turnover of recordings is very rapid, so there is little point in arranging by a detailed classification. Once again, as with catalogue numbers, this arrangement by broad groups in browser boxes has the advantage of familiarity, as users will be used to the same method in record shops. Simple arrangement by composer as an alternative can be used.

It would be possible to arrange records by the classification in use for scores and books, but this would not be easy as so many records are issued with more than one work, each quite often in a different form and by a different composer. As far as is known, only Liverpool Music Library has attempted to do this. Bliss made provision for such an idea in BC, however.

Records are not easy to consult when they are filed on ordinary shelves, as they would need to be if arranged by a close classification. The browser boxes make selection easier. In arranging by the broad classification, when a record includes two or three works one of these will have to be selected as the most likely to be sought. For records with more than three works it is probably best to have a group called 'collections' under instrumental and vocal.

A possible arrangement for browser boxes for display of classical records in sleeves, or the sleeves only might be:
Instrumental
Collections
Orchestral

Symphonies
Concertos
Chamber music
Sonatas and pieces for solo instruments.
Vocal
Collections
Sacred choral
Secular choral
Opera
Songs
A similar arrangement could be used for cassettes in racks or on shelves.

For popular forms the arrangement can be very similar. The primary division needs to be into form of music:
Folk
Country and western
Jazz
Rock
Progressive pop
Brass band
etc.
Under each form the material can be arranged alphabetically by name(s) of performer(s) or groups.

If a library has a record or cassette loan collection it must make it easily available. The fewer barriers to use the better. In this particular situation commercial display has established a habit of use, with which the library user is familiar. To use the same system breaks down the barriers. Too elaborate a classification or indicator system would only have the opposite effect.

Archive collections will almost certainly be closed access with only the staff allowed to handle the records. Here again arrangement by the trade catalogue numbers would seem to be the simplest method.

CHAPTER SEVEN

CONCLUSION

THE EARLIER CHAPTERS have been concerned with the existing classification schemes and some problems in various aspects of the classification of music. It is evident even from a very limited examination such as this that there is a very wide variety of methods which can be employed in organising a music library. It is as well that there should be, for there are many different ways of approach to the art of music, and libraries must attempt to cater for all of them.

It is customary for the music librarian to have both knowledge of the subject and professional skill. Some even argue that the latter is unnecessary and that it is preferable to employ musicians as librarians. If there is a choice between a musician and a librarian without interest in music, it will probably be safer to choose the latter, but it is not unreasonable to expect librarians to have both subject and professional knowledge, and there are many good music librarians who started their careers with the skills of librarianship and an enthusiasm for music, yet without a knowledge of its techniques, which they have acquired later. It is this love of their subject which will probably prevent music librarians of any kind from falling into the trap of becoming too concerned with the 'how' of their work and forgetting the 'why'.

The aim in organising any material must always be simplicity, so that if possible readers remain unaware of *how* they have been helped to find what they want. With this in mind, many music librarians break away from a classified subject arrangement on their shelves in arranging scores while using a classification for the literature. Instead, they prefer to classify scores by physical format. Thus there will be separate sequences of vocal scores, full scores, bound instrumental scores and miniature scores. Some libraries, such as the Central Music Library, arrange much of their instrumental music according to the instrument, unbound in pamphlet boxes. Such an arrangement might offend the keen librarian who likes everything neatly ordered, but it is very practical, easy to use and familiar to the reader, who will almost certainly have met the same method in music shops. Bound instrumental scores arranged on the shelves are classified by instrument, but vocal, full and miniature scores are best arranged alphabetically by composer within each sequence.

County libraries and other libraries which loan choral, orchestral and chamber sets, seem to find the easiest classification to be by these broad groups, sub-arranged by composer. Here again pamphlet boxes are very convenient for storage.

These methods are simple because they recognise physical differences, which in this case are more important than subject differences, and because they suit the approach of most readers. They will work in any kind of music library. The enquiry is usually by composer and, in the case of libraries loaning sets, the material is only handled by the staff, so this system is practical.

As has been stated, the literature will be arranged by a subject classification. This different approach to the two types of material presents no problem, even with DC where, according to the scheme, scores and books are arranged together, as the classification can be used for the literature and not for the scores. Some libraries have a curious practice of classifying the scores even when they are arranged alphabetically by composer and a dictionary catalogue is used.

In selecting the scheme to be used, choice should be based, as shown in chapter one, on an analysis of four factores—time, money, people and material. For complete coverage of western classical music it would be difficult to better the BCM scheme. With the addition of the Langridge schedules for jazz it offers even wider scope and will meet the needs of most libraries.

FURTHER READING

THE TITLES CITED in this list are not intended to provide a comprehensive survey, but to serve as pointers for further study. With that in mind an asterisk has been used to indicate those titles which themselves have bibliographies or reading lists.

It is hoped to include a comprehensive bibliography of the classification, cataloguing, indexing and bibliographical control of music in the second volume.

KEEPING UP TO DATE
Periodicals
Brio
Fontes artis musicae
Notes
Abstracts
Library and information science abstracts (LISA)
Répertoire international de littérature musicale (RILM)
Any good music library should stock all five of the above titles, although a special library not part of a bigger library might not take LISA.

GENERAL STUDIES
Bryant, E T *Music librarianship* London, Clarke, 1959. New edition to be published very shortly.

*Langridge, Derek *Classification and indexing in the humanities* London, Butterworth, 1976.

*Langridge, Derek *Approach to classification for students of librarianship* London, Bingley; Hamden, Conn, Linnet, 1973.

*Maltby, Arthur *Classification in the 1970's: a second look* rev ed, London, Bingley; Hamden, Conn, Linnet, 1976.

*Needham, C D *Organising knowledge in libraries* 2nd ed London, Deutsch, 1971.

MUSIC CLASSIFICATION
*The classification of music and literature on music: a survey of practice in several countries' *Fontes artis musicae* XV, 1968, 83–102.

Coates, Eric 'The British catalogue of music classification' *Music libraries and instruments* London, Hinrichsen, 1961, 156–165.

Line, Maurice B 'A classification for music on historical principles' *Libri* 12(4) 1962, 352–363.

Ott, Alfons 'The role of music in public libraries of medium size' *Music libraries and instruments* London, Hinrichsen, 1961, 79–83.

THE SCHEMES

Acknowledgement is made to the compilers, editors and publishers of these for the use of extracts from the schedules and instructions where appropriate.

Special

Coates, Eric *The British catalogue of music classification* London, BNB, 1960. For Langridge extension for jazz see article below.

Bradley, Carol June *The Dickinson classification: a cataloguing and classification manual for music* Carlisle, Pennsylvania, Carlisle Books, 1968.

Systematik der Musikliteratur und der Musikalien für öffentliche Music-buchereien Reutlingen, Verlag Bucherei und Bildung, 1963.

Pethes, Ivan *A flexible classification system of music and literature on music* Budapest, Centre of Library Science and Methodology, 1967. Preprint.

Ott, Alfons. For this scheme see article cited above.

General schemes

BC: Bliss, Henry Evelyn *A bibliographic classification* New York, Wilson, 1953. 3 vols. Revised edition in progress edited by Jack Mills and Vanda Broughton. London, Butterworth, 1977–.

Brown: Brown, James Duff *Subject classification 3rd ed* London, Grafton, 1939.

Colon: Ranganathan, S R *Colon classification 6th ed* Bombay, Asia Publishing House, 1960.

DC: Dewey, Melvil *Decimal classification 18th ed* New York, Forest Press, 1971. 3 vols. Phoenix 780 Music compiled by Russell Sweeney and John Clews (MS limited circulation).

LC: Library of Congress *Classification: Class M music and books on music. 2nd ed* Washington, Library of Congress, 1917.

UDC: Universal decimal classification. English full edition: UDC 78 music. London, British Standards Institution, 1971.

Classification of jazz

Langridge, Derek 'Classifying the literature of jazz' *Brio* 4(1), 1967, 2–6. Extension to BCM.

Langridge, Derek *Your jazz collection* London, Bingley; Hamden, Conn, Archon, 1970.

Instruments

Hornbostel, E M and Sachs, C 'Classification of musical instruments' translated from the original Germany by Anthony Baines and Klaus P Wachsmann *Galpin Society journal* 14, 1961, 3–29.

Music bibliographies arranged systematically

Altmann, Wilhelm *Kammermusik-Katalog* Leipzig, Hofmeister, 1945.

Altmann, Wilhelm *Orchester-Literatur-Katalog* Leipzig, Leuckart, two volumes, 1926-36.

Becker, Carl Ferdinand *Systematisch-chronologische Darstellung der Musikalischen Literatur* Amsterdam, Knuf, 1964 (reprint of the original 1836 edition).

Richter, Johannes F *Kammermusik-Katalog* Leipzig, Hofmeister, 1960.

INDEX

Acoustics: Treatment in DC, LC and Colon compared 49-50

Alternative treatment: Bliss Bibliographic Classification 70

Altmann, Wilhelm: Classification scheme 46-7

Alphabetical order 12, 98; McColvin 62

Analysis, Subject 14-22; see also Citation order

Arrangements: Classification BCM 30-1. Dickinson Classification 37, 38, 40 41; LC 52; McColvin 62; UDC 64, 67

Auxiliaries: UDC 65-6

Auxiliary tables: BCM 25-6, 30, 31, 32, 33; Pethes 45

BBC music library: Chamber music Catalogue: Classification 46-7

Bliss Bibliographic Classification (BC) 10; 49, 50, 69-76, 87, 94 revision by Jack Mills 72-6, 87

Books: Classification see Literature: Classification

British Catalogue of Music Classification (BCM) 10, 11, 19, 23-36, 87, 98; LC 50; Phoenix 780 58, 59; McColvin 61; BC 70, 71; BC revision 72, 73, 75, 76; Brown 78

British Standards Institution: UDC 63

Brown Subject Classification 49, 50, 72, 77-80

Cassettes: Classification see Recordings: Classification

Catalogues 12, 13

Central music library (Westminster): Arrangement of scores 97

Chamber music: Treatment in SMM and McColvin compared 43; Altmann 46-7; see also Instrumental music

Citation order 20-1; BCM 26-33; Dickinson scheme 38; Pethes 45; LC (instrumental music) 52; LC (vocal music) 53; Phoenix 780 59; UDC 64, 66; BC 72; BC revision 72-3; Langridge 84

Clewes, John: Phoenix 780 58

Coates, Eric J: BCM 10, 24, 72

Colon Classification 49, 80-2

Combination order see Citation order

Compound subjects 19-21 and passim individual schemes

Computers 11

Cost effectiveness 11, 12

103

Dewey Decimal Classification (DC) 10, 11, 19, 49, 50, 55-63, 87, 98; LC 64; Brown 77, 78
Dickinson Classification 23, 36-42
Discs: Classification see Recordings: Classification

Enumerative classification 19-20
Ethnomusicology: Pethes 45; Phoenix 780 59-61; BC revision 73-5; Hornbostel-Sachs 87-91

Faceted classification 10
Facets 14-22 and passim individual schemes
Financial considerations 11, 12
Flexible classification (Pethes) 43-6
Foci see Facets
Folk music 18, 83; Phoenix 780 60; UDC 69
Format, physical: Scores: Arrangement by 17, 34, 97-8

General classification schemes 49-82
German classification schemes 42-3

Hornbostel-Sachs classification for instruments 87-91; Phoenix 780 60-1

Instrumental music: Classification: BCM 25, 28-31; Dickinson 39-41; Ott 42; SMM 42-3; Pethes 44-5; Altmann 46-7; LC 52; DC 57-8; McColvin 62; UDC 65, 67, 68-9; BC 71-2; BC revision 75, 76; Brown 78-9; Colon 81; Hornbostel-Sachs 87-91; recordings 94-5

Instrumentalists: Use of libraries 13
Instruments 87-91; comparison of treatment in classification schemes 87
International Association of Music Libraries 63, 91; Classification subcommission 42, 44, 46; United Kingdom Branch 24; West German Branch 42-3

Jazz: Classification 11, 98; BCM 33-6; Pethes 45; LC 55; DC 57, 58; Phoenix 780 60; McColvin 63; UDC 69; BC 71; BC revision 74; Langridge 83-6

Langridge, Derek: Jazz: BCM 33-6, 98; Phoenix 780 60; BC revision 74-5; own scheme 83-6
Library of Congress Classification (LC) 11, 19, 49, 50-5, 87; BCM 23; Dickinson 37; BC 70, 71, 72
Literature: Music 17; BCM 24, 27, 32; SMM 43; Pethes 44; LC 55; DC 56-8; Phoenix 780 59; McColvin 62-3; UDC 64-9; BC 70-2; BC revision 72-5; Brown 78-80; Colon 80-1
Liverpool music library: Arrangement of recordings 94

McColvin Classification 23, 43, 61-3
Mills, Jack: BC revision 72
Music librarians: Qualifications 97
Musical instruments 87-91; Comparison of treatment in classification schemes 87
Musicologists: Use of libraries 13

Notation: Classification see passim individual schemes

Ott, Dr Alfons: Classification scheme 42

Pethes, Ivan: Classification scheme 43-6
Parts: Arrangement in libraries 98: Dickinson 37; UDC 69;
Performers: Use of libraries 13, 14
Phase relationships 17, 19, 22; BC revision 73; Langridge 84, 85
Phoenix 780: Dewey Decimal Classification 10, 56, 58-61, 72, 75, 86, 87
Physical format: Scores: Arrangement by 17, 34, 97-8
Popular music 11, 83; Phoenix 780 60; McColvin 63; BC 71; BC revision 74-5; recordings 95

Ranganathan, Dr S R 14, 24, 72, 80
Readers' needs 13, 97-8; Dickinson Classification 37; Pethes 45

Recordings: Classification 93-5: BC 70; Langridge 85-6

SMM Classification scheme 42-3
Sachs, Curt see Hornbostel-Sachs Classification
Scores: Classification 17, 97-8; BCM 24-33; Dickinson 36-42; Ott 42; SMM 42-3; Altmann 46-7; LC 51-3; DC 56-8; Phoenix 780 59; McColvin 61-2; UDC 64-9; BC 71-2, 73, 76; Brown 78-80; Colon 81
Sheet music: Arrangement in libraries 17, 97
Sound recordings: Classification see Recordings: Classification
Singers: Use of libraries 14
Special classification schemes 23-47
Staff: Cost 12-13; qualifications 97
Subject analysis 14-22 see also Citation order
Sweeney, Russell: Phoenix 780 58

Teachers: Use of libraries 13

Universal Decimal Classification (UDC) 45, 63-9, 87
Users' needs 13, 97-8: Dickinson Classification 37; Pethes 45

Vocal music 21; BCM 24, 27, 29, 31-2; Dickinson scheme 39-41; Ott Classification 42; SMM 42-3; Pethes 44-5; Altmann 46-7; LC 52-3; DC 57; McColvin 61-2; UDC 65-8; BC 71; BC revision 75, 76; Brown 79-80; Colon 81; recordings 95